# INUKSUIT

# I N U K S

# U I T

## SILENT MESSENGERS OF THE ARCTIC

## NORMAN HALLENDY

### WITH PHOTOGRAPHS BY THE AUTHOR

DOUGLAS & McINTYRE
VANCOUVER / TORONTO

UNIVERSITY OF WASHINGTON PRESS
SEATTLE

Douglas & McIntyre Ltd.
2323 Quebec Street, Suite 201
Vancouver, British Columbia  V5T 4S7
Canada

Canadian Cataloguing in Publication Data
Hallendy, Norman, 1932–
Inuksuit
    Includes bibliographical references and index.
    ISBN 1-55054-778-X
1. Inuksuit.  2. Inuit—Antiquities.  3. Canada, Northern—Antiquities.  I. Title.
E99.E7H24 2000      306'.089'9712071      C00-910074-1

Originated in Canada by Douglas & McIntyre and published in the United States of America by The University of Washington Press, PO Box 50096, Seattle, WA 98145-5096.

Library of Congress Cataloging-in-Publication Data

Hallendy, Norman.
    Inuksuit : silent messengers of the Arctic / Norman Hallendy with photographs by the author.
        p. cm.
    Includes biographical references and index.
    ISBN 0-295-97983-6 (alk. paper)
    1. Inuit—Material culture. 2. Inuit—Rites and ceremonies. 3. Inuit—Antiquities.
4. Stone—Arctic regions. 5. Building stones—Arctic regions. 6. Stone carving—Arctic regions.
7. Arctic regions—Antiquities. I. Title.

E99.E7 H226 2000
971.9'01—DC21                           00-028661

Editing by Saeko Usukawa
Design by George Vaitkunas
Maps by Eric Leinberger
Jacket photographs by Norman Hallendy: *front*, a beautiful inuksuk at a revered site near Saatturittuq, southwest Baffin Island; *back*, twilight after a storm at Inuksugalait
Printed and bound by C & C Offset Printing Co. Ltd. in Hong Kong
Printed on acid-free paper

We gratefully acknowledge the financial support of the Canada Council for the Arts, the British Columbia Ministry of Tourism, Small Business and Culture, and the Government of Canada through the Book Publishing Industry Development Program (BPIDP) for our publishing activities.

Pages 2 and 3: The hauntingly beautiful site at Inuksugalait, where ancient *inuksuit* have stood for countless generations, southwest Baffin Island.

Page 6: An *inuksuk inuktaqarniraijuq*, an inuksuk-like figure that symbolizes the presence of humans, to inform whalers of a meeting place, southwest Baffin Island.

# DEDICATION

I dedicate these words and thoughts to you, Angajukak. I travelled in the safety of your company to places I had never seen. I discovered what it meant to be human at the side of a dying caribou. I remember the night we were snug in our tent and the little baby farted. You said, "Listen, listen my son, you have just heard the sound of life." And we laughed and laughed.

Tears come to my eyes when I think of the sounds of our laughing and the touch of your breath.

Taima, Angajukak.

# CONTENTS

# INTRODUCTION:
# THE SENSE OF WONDER

ONE SUNNY SEPTEMBER AFTERNOON, the door to our classroom swung open and in walked our new geography teacher. Offering nothing by way of recognition, Captain du Marbois ambled across the floor toward the slate blackboard that covered the top half of one wall. He picked up a piece of chalk and, with the flow and elegance of a skilled calligrapher, began to write:

> Far to the north in a land called Svithiod
> Is a mountain one thousand miles high.
> Once in a thousand years a raven comes
> To sharpen her beak.
> When the mountain has been worn smooth
> With the surface of the earth
> A moment of eternity will have passed.

Tossing the chalk back onto the blackboard's wooden track, Captain du Marbois studied us with a faint smile. Then he turned and strode out the door; it was another week before we saw him again.

This remarkable man was a retired sea captain whose life was one unending and event-filled voyage. He had returned from the sea to devote his remaining years to teaching in a boys' school. But rather than deploying exercises, lessons and reading assignments, the captain revived our sense of wonder. He mesmerized us with his experiences as a twelve-year-old cabin boy struggling around the Horn in sailing ships. Once, in the middle of an account of a cannibal feast in Borneo, he stopped as if to snatch a floating thought from the air and asked whether we knew the meaning of the equation $E=MC^2$. Observing a room of bewildered faces, he proceeded to acquaint us with the virtues of Transcendental Meditation.

Each moment in his class was filled with some new and often astounding adventure, tale or insight that awakened the curiosity within all of us. By sharing his quests and fears, the captain caused us to wonder not just about mysteries in distant lands but about matters in our own lives. Never cease wondering, he admonished us, for wonder defines the path to discovery.

Since that September day so long ago, my classmates have graduated to become doctors, politicians, artists, lawyers, mechanics, teachers. Some of us moved to distant lands, others never left the place of our childhood. Eventually, old Captain du Marbois died and became a memory. But to this day, we continue to search, in our way, for Svithiod.

*Inuksuit: Silent Messengers of the Arctic* is one reflection of such a search. It is a true story that began unfolding since my first encounter with Inuit elders in 1958, the year I arrived in Cape Dorset (now called Kinngait), on the tip of southwest Baffin Island, working for the Department of Nothern Affairs and National Resources. Coming into the Arctic at this period made it possible to befriend the Inummariit— the real people, those who know how to live on the land in the manner of their ancestors. To them, I must have appeared as a young, white outsider who had the courtesy to smile, nod hello and lend a hand without being asked. By the time I headed home at the end of that first summer, several elders recognized me with a smile and a *"Qanuipit?"*: How are you?

I suspect many were amused by my asking permission to take photographs of them. When I returned to the North the next year, I brought copies of each picture I had taken and gave one to the elders I had photographed, which pleased them greatly. I also had a photo album to show pictures of my family, dog, birthday parties and other captured domestic moments. The album helped establish me as a friend.

Soon, we were not only exchanging *"Qanuipit?"* but genuine handshakes. Certain elders, especially those whose spouses were dead and who lived alone, began asking me to visit them, which I happily did. I always brought with me a little food or a small gift. Eventually, my visits became occasions for an elder to talk about the "old days" or some specific event that resonated in them. It was natural for me to enquire about details and points of clarification. In this sense, the get-togethers were never question-and-answer sessions but genuine encounters shared by friends.

This book was born of such encounters. It is not meant to be a treatise on traditional Inuit life; by necessity, such an important work would best be written by one who has truly experienced the joys and hardships of living on the land in the traditional manner. The Inuit have survived for more than four thousand years in the elemental world of the Arctic, where temperatures fluctuate between extremes of −60 and 30 degrees Celsius (−22 to 86 degrees F). For traditional Inuit, survival meant adapting perfectly to the environment and using what it offered—blocks of snow for winter shelter, and stone, skin, ivory and bone as the foundation of their material culture. It was a life forever on the edge, and several elders I knew well offered accounts of unspeakable hardship and the dark side of human experience. But they were more eager to share their joy of living on the land: of the hunt, of a son's first seal, of happy feasts and of the elation felt from having survived a brush with death or, better yet, from the warm embrace of one's mate on a winter's night. In so doing, they evoked in me a deeper perception of life, theirs and mine.

Such a gift, for that is what I have been given by the elders these past forty years, continues to be a source of wonder. I have learned, for example, that there is a great advantage to growing old with those who share a wealth of memories. Passing through the veil of inhibition, we can engage in leisured speculation of intimate subjects, such as ecstasy or death, and discuss matters of a painful nature without discomfort or shame.

This book is my attempt to faithfully render the insights, impressions and experiences of those remarkable and generous Inuit elders who had lived in an unforgiving yet beguiling world, at a time when the earth was considered a great living being. In their company, I learned of the existence of both a physical and a spiritual landscape. The elders spoke of places of power and objects of veneration that defined the very soul of the world they knew. In many ways, they define the soul of the world you and I know, as well. Perhaps, after reading their words, the constellations in your night sky and the grains of sand on your beach may never seem quite the same.

One of my closest friends, Issuhungituq, once asked, "For whom are you writing these words?" I answered, "I'm writing them for you and me." Issuhungituq, whose name means eternity, was happy. And now, each year when I visit her final resting place, I whisper, "Issuhungituq, I'm not yet finished."

I feel her presence in everything around me.

Kuujjuaraapik
(Great Whale River)

Umiujaq • Sanikiluaq • *Hudson Bay*

QUEBEC

Inukjuak •

Puvirniqtuuq
(Povungnituk) •

Kuujjuaq
(Fort Chimo) •

Akulivik •
Salluit • Ivujivik

sualujjuaq
akem Bay) •

*Hudson Strait*

Kinngait
(Cape Dorset)

Salliq
(Coral Harbour)

Southampton I

Kimmiruk
(Lake Harbour) • Ammaarjuaq • Seekuseelak
(Foxe Peninsula)

Naujaat/Aivilik
(Repulse Bay)

Iqaluit
(Frobisher Bay)

Sanirajaq
(Hall Beach) • Iglulik
(Igloolik)

Arvilikjuaq
(Pelly Bay)

Uqsuqtuuq
(Gjoa Haven)

Pangnirtuuq
(Pangnirtung)

*Nettilling
Lake*

Talurjuaq/Taloyoak
(Spence Bay)

Qikiqtarjuaq
(Broughton Island)

Baffin Island

N U N A V U T

Kangiq&ugaapik
(Clyde River)

Mittimatalik/Tununiq
(Pond Inlet)

Ikpiarjuk/Tununirusiq
(Arctic Bay)

Qausuittuq
(Resolute Bay)

Ausuittuq
(Grise Fiord)

KALAALIT NUNAAT
(GREENLAND)

Ellesmere
Island

Arviat/Arviatjuaq (Eskimo Point)

Tikirarjuaq (Whale Cove)

Igluligaarjuk
(Chesterfield Inlet)

Kangiq&iniq (Rankin Inlet)

Qamanittuaq
(Baker Lake)

DISTRICT OF
KEEWATIN

Qingauq
(Bathurst Inlet)

NORTHWEST
TERRITORIES

Umingmaktuuq

Qurluqtuuq
(Coppermine)

Whitehorse •

Iqaluktuuttiaq
(Cambridge Bay)

YUKON

Victoria
Island

Paulatuuq
(Paulatuk)

Ulukhaqtuuq
(Holman)

Tuktuujaqtuuq
(Tuktoyaktuk)

Inuvik •

Banks
Island

Ikaahuk
(Sachs Harbour)

Ak&aavik
(Aklavik)

Old
Crow

BAFFIN ISLAND

Nurrata

Akitsiraqvik

SEEKUSEELAK

SEEKUSEELAK (Foxe Peninsula)

Inuksugalait

Kangisuriuq
(Andrew Gordon Bay)

SUC
REC

REGION

Saatturittuq
(Sartoweetuk)

Itiliardjuk

Sarko

Kiaqtuq

Tellik Inlet

Mallik

Kinngait (Cape Dorset)

Qujaligiaqtubic

Seekuseelak (Foxe Peninsula) on Baffin Island.
Only the place names mentioned in the text
are shown. There are, in fact, hundreds of places
along this coast; every ancient site, cove island,
and natural feature has a name.

Hudson Strait

# INUKSUIT

FROM THE RUGGED MOUNTAINS IN THE EAST TO THE
VAST TUNDRA IN THE WEST IS A PLACE SOME CALL ARCTIC
AND OTHERS CALL NUNATSIAQ, MEANING "THE BEAUTIFUL LAND."

Icy mountains
sail the arctic seas
of Hudson Strait.

Remnants of the last ice age
lie silently upon the mountains
of Baffin Island.

Stretching to the horizon
are endless prairies of tundra
in the interior of
southwest Baffin Island.

Carved by time are spectacular fiords
such as this one at
Pangnirtuuq, Baffin Island.

Upon the return of the
sun in spring, the earth receives
its first water, Kinngait area.

In little more than
a handful of poor soil,
life emerges each summer,
north Baffin Island.

During a time that southerners call summer,
darkness is replaced by a haunting twilight,
southwest Baffin Island.

# FIRST ENCOUNTERS

IMAGINE A VAST and powerful landscape stretching to infinity in all directions. You are at the centre of this world, a place where you can walk on the surface of a frozen sea to distant islands or to favoured locations of animals you must kill in order to live. You have been travelling alone on foot for several days. The only sound you hear is made by your movement, your breathing and the occasional gust of wind. Alone in the deepest sense, you find yourself atop a barren hill and are rewarded with an unobstructed view of the horizon that encircles you. There is no single vanishing point.

Tracing with your eyes the precise line where heaven meets earth, you reflect on the insignificance of your presence. Your journey across this vast expanse is also a journey of the mind. What you yearn to see, you begin to imagine; what you cannot imagine, you encounter unexpectedly. At first, you see what appears to be nothing more than a speck in the distance. Soon it creates a focal point, moving you from the centre of your universe to its periphery. As the distance closes, you are compelled to stop, transfixed by an ancient message left upon the landscape. Stone upon lichen-encrusted stone, it is an *inuksuk*, the signature of an Arctic hunter who passed this way on a journey that would last a lifetime. Who was he? Where did he come from? Where was he going?

You marvel at the perfect balance of stones selected and arranged with great care. The size of a young boy, the inuksuk, its mere presence attaching you to its unknown builder, warms you with its sense of humanity. As thanks, you leave a piece of your precious food tucked between its lower stones and move on. Only you know what you said to it the moment before parting. Soon you meet another inuksuk, and another. You are no longer alone.

❧ ❧ ❧

MY NAME IS APIRSUQTI, the inquisitive one. It was given to me some four decades ago by Inuit elders whom I met at a time when they were leaving their life on the land and beginning the struggle to find a different one in various communities established by the Canadian government throughout the Arctic.

I was given the name when I had the strength and vigour of my youth, when everything seemed possible, when life felt like an endless journey, a miracle celebrated each morning in my first conscious breath. It was a time when I first began to view the Arctic from the vantage provided by elders who would influence how I saw myself and the world around me for the rest of my life.

Simeonie Quppapik, one of my mentors, was the first to inform me of my Inuktitut *atig*, or name. It was from Simeonie, who shared songs and stories of life when the Inuit were *nunaliriniq*, at one with the land, that I first learned about the ancient stone figures of the Arctic. I remember the time when Simeonie pointed to one far in the distance. "Its name is inuksuk," he informed me. "It means that which acts in the capacity of a human. Some were placed upon the land by our ancestors, but others were here before us. There are *inuksuit* [plural of inuksuk] that were built by the ancient ones we call the Tunniit, who came and prepared the land for all of us." Simeonie turned and looked at me. "Look around you, Apirsuqti," he said, radiating a wide and warm smile. "Look at the hills, the sea, the inuksuit everywhere. We are all made of the same stuff. We all possess a spirit, only the way we are arranged temporarily separates us."

"Will you help me understand what these inuksuit mean?" I asked.

Simeonie replied he would, but that first I had to try and understand their meaning on my own.

And so began my Arctic journeys with the silent messengers called inuksuit. I found them along the seacoast and on hilltops, near ancient sites, at places that were dangerous to travellers and where, in traditional times, people had to show respect or suffer the ire of malefic spirits. I found them on southwest Baffin Island and in the central and western Arctic. I was informed of their presence in Alaska and Greenland, now called Kalaallit Nunaat. I heard of similar figures existing in other parts of the world.

Over the years, I was taught how to understand the many different messages of inuksuit. Some would indicate the location of a safe harbour or a dangerous passage. To a hunter, they revealed where food was cached, where migrating animals tended to be at certain times of the year or where preferred routes had their beginnings. Some stone markers placed on the landscape pointed the way to a spring hidden from view, to the entrance to a narrow pass or to a natural shelter that could be used in time of dire need. And some were objects of veneration.

Eventually, I acquired a detailed image in my mind of a number of inuksuit and their locations. They became reference points from which I could depart and return with confidence. Now, I can recall where they stand as well as the conditions that prevailed when I first encountered them; who I was with and who told of their meaning. In this way, I have become attached to the very thought of inuksuit, to families and elders, and, in some unfathomable way, to the ancient hunters who built them.

How can this be so? How can a pile of stones have such power over the mind? For the Inummariit—those who lived on the land in the manner of their ancestors—the sinew of their world was the oral tradition, a graphic language made up of stories, images and vital geographic and cultural information that was passed from parent to child, from generation to generation. Within this spare world, one devoid of writing instruments, inuksuit were the material forms of the oral tradition. They created a profile in space. As an outsider, I realized that I could never hope to understand inuksuit without first understanding this cultural context.

Such an understanding was acquired slowly by returning each year to spend time with elders and friends. While I visited the North in all seasons, I found my journeys during the season we call summer often yielded the richest stories. It was the time when the sun descended to momentarily touch the distant hills, only to quickly rise again and move in a great circle around us, attaching each day to the next by a band of twilight. Summer was two seasons: the first, the elders called *siangiyaut*, which means when young ducks preen; and the second, *saggat*, which means when caribou have short hair. This was when men hunted seals, walrus and caribou. It was when women and children gathered edible seaweed, berries and eggs, and hunted rabbits and birds.

Summer was also the all too brief period when the Inuit lived in tents and each night told or listened to wonderful tales. Storytelling was a form of communion as well as entertainment. It brought the past into the present. It connected children to their ancestors. It filled the tent with images that danced in the imagination. Sometimes, these stories cast a sombre spell when they revealed great hardship or terrible suffering. Such tales would often be brought to a conclusion by the ancient expression *ajurnarmat*, it cannot be helped.

The stories or recounting of events were often told without embellishment. Words were selected and arranged so as to create lucid pictures in the listener's mind. A story was not simply heard, it was seen. I remember Simeonie describing a horrible event in the space of just a few words. Looking up from the sleeping platform, he recalled: "When I was still a boy, my father and his hunting companions came back to the camp with walrus meat. We were joyful. But no one in our family ate any meat, we were full. The next day those who had eaten the meat were sick, dying or dead. In a rage, my father took up his rifle and shot each lump of meat . . . and each piece began to move!"

Among the many elders I met, some became as close to me as uncles, aunts or grandparents. Addressing them as such was a matter of respect, thus further strengthening the bond between us. Even the memory of their names—Anirniq, Ikuma and Issuhungituq (spirit, fire and eternity)—reminds me of the countless times I was humbled by their perceptions and kindness.

Travelling with them exposed me in an intimate way to their joy at being back on the land, as well as to their world, including the many meanings of inuksuit. It was my great fortune that these perceptions, along with their words and expressions, now seldom used and in some cases no longer understood, were shared with me. I learned that it was not unmanly to be moved by the touch, smell and sounds of the land. This sensual communion, this *unganaqtuq nuna* (deep and total attachment to the land), is often expressed in spiritual terms. I am unable to forget how an old woman spoke quietly of *nuna*'s (the land's) fearsome, deadly and divine qualities with equal reverence. In one encounter, I asked her, "Tell me, *anannatsiak* (grandmother), what was the most terrible thing in your life?"

She looked into my eyes. "My childhood," she whispered. "We were often hungry and sometimes starving."

In an attempt to dispel her painful memories, I quickly asked, "What was the most beautiful place you remember?"

She once more looked into my eyes and, with a faint smile, whispered, "The place where I lived during my childhood."

⟩ ⟩ ⟩

THERE WERE ELDERS who tolerated my seemingly endless questions and who somehow found pleasure in our company. They became my mentors. Elders such as Pingwortuk, Oshutsiak Pudlat, Simeonie Quppapik, Pauta Saila and Osuitok Ipeelee, among others, taught me how to see the land and the inuksuit on it, in a literal and metaphorical sense. Nothing in my previous experience could prepare me for what was about to come. And I had yet to learn Pingwortuk's secret for staying alive.

Pingwortuk was the first to take me out on the land, an expression that often means going out to sea. Compact and deceptively strong, Ping, as his friends called him, had hands that were as gnarled as ancient arctic willows yet as dextrous as those of any artist. His face looked like well-tanned leather, for he was out on his boat as often as weather permitted.

Ping's name means a gentle and friendly plaything, and in fact he was well known for his jovial manner and delightful countenance—he was like a smile on two feet—qualities that obscured the fact that he was a serious and competent hunter and trapper. His laughter, especially following some antic that caused him injury, was infectious. "Laughter," he said, "is very good when things are bad."

But his laughter was not reserved for hard times. Ping was completely at ease with the Qallunaat, the white men, who often sought him out for help, guidance and the use of his boat. One day we were out hunting seal with a well-known writer from New York City. Unfortunately for the writer, there were no seals to be had. As the day wore on, one finally emerged near the boat, dove back into the water and then returned to the surface, where it was met by our hail of bullets. The seal seemed to elude us for quite some time until it finally swam away. I don't believe our guest from New York City ever realized that our elusive prey was, in fact, a stone-cold dead seal. Ping's mischievous helper had rigged the animal with fishing lines and had played it like a puppet.

Ping had a contemplative side as well, which I glimpsed during a trip to the West Foxe Islands. He would spend much time staring out to sea, watching the erratic flight of sea pigeons or gazing at the clouds. Ping seemed to adore everything around him when he was on the water. The last time I was with Ping, in fact, was when we were far out at sea on a glorious day. The sea was so calm it appeared as if we were drifting on the reflected clouds. For some inexplicable reason, I asked: "Ping, if we knew that we would never see one another again, what words would you give me to remember you by?"

He offered his gentle smile. "I'll give you the secret for staying alive," he said. "Always keep yourself in the position where you will be able to take advantage of that which is about to happen." I never saw him again. His earthly journeys came to a quiet end the following year.

Oshutsiak was very different from Ping. He was a quiet man, lightly built and often wrapped in deep thought. He was one of three brothers, all highly respected artists. Oshutsiak figured he was born around 1908, in the Ammaarjuak region of southwest Baffin Island. As with everyone else of his generation, the time of his birth was not a calendar date but a personal event that related to some other more important occurrence. For example, they might refer to the time of birth as the time of the great hunger or the time when the great ship from the South arrived.

Oshutsiak was never effusive in his greetings or farewells. Seeing me for the first time after a year, he would raise his eyebrows ever so slightly—a subtle sign of approval—make me a cup of tea, look straight into my eyes and, with a faint smile, wait for me to make the first move. He would watch me as a raven would watch some mildly interesting subject.

Though I was familiar with the belief in spirits before I met Oshutsiak, he gave me the opportunity to go beyond an introduction. He believed in the existence of spirits and that their vitality still infused all the places where they were known to dwell. In a burst of intense creativity, Oshutsiak would draw the spirits with whom he was familiar and sell the art to earn some money. Southerners would buy his work, thinking they had purchased a quaint fantasy. At the same time, I can still remember when we exchanged glances in Kinngait's little Anglican church on Sunday mornings. Oshutsiak, who spoke so reverently about spirits and metaphysical landscapes, was a devout Christian, as were all the other elders whom I knew.

Simeonie, Oshutsiak's adopted brother, claimed he was born twice. The first time was when his mother's midwife brought him into the world. That was when whalers began visiting the area where he was born. The second time was when the Canadian government said he was born, which a bureaucrat determined to be in 1909, duly written on an important piece of paper. In either case, he was adopted out as a very young child.

Simeonie was bright and inquisitive, and had his likeness captured on film in 1923 at age fourteen by the legendary American film-maker Robert Flaherty. At the time, Flaherty was given the name White Swan by the Inuit with whom he lived. One of Simeonie's relatives, the beautiful Glass Nose, was White Swan's girlfriend and likely influenced him to photograph members of her family before he headed back South. I've often looked at that sweet photograph, then looked at one taken when Simeonie was a strong and handsome hunter. In later years, I would turn and see a small and delicate man, who had not wielded a harpoon for some time. Until the end, though, Simeonie had a remarkable memory. He could still sing the songs he had learned many years ago when he lived in skin tents and snow-houses while growing up at Ammaarjuak, the land of the ancient sod houses.

Pauta possesses a different strength, the strength of presence. He stands tall, looks you straight in the eye and assumes the dominant position. His smile is knowing rather than engaging. A master carver whose works are in major collections throughout the world, Pauta believes he was born in 1916 near Nurrata; now deserted, it was one of the oldest permanent camps on southwest Baffin Island. His father, Saila, was a powerful camp boss who some believed had the powers of a shaman. It is said Saila could kill a walrus with a single thrust of a harpoon. While Pauta may not have inherited his father's powers, he did possess a passionate reverence for the land. In the evening, when we were all in the tent, he would often sit by the entrance with hands folded and a faint smile on his face. Then, unexpectedly, he would softly sing to himself some ancient song. While we went about our business, Pauta would make his personal journeys through time.

Osuitok remains one of the most important people in my life. He befriended me the first time I set foot in Kinngait (Cape Dorset), and he has been my mentor for more than thirty-five years. Osuitok was born near Kinngait in 1923 and lived in various camps along the Foxe Peninsula of Baffin Island. The area is known as Seekuseelak, a name that means "where there is open water in winter." It is a remarkable place—one of the most mysterious in the eastern Arctic—where there are traces of human habitation reaching back thousands of years.

One of the finest carvers in Canada, Osuitok seems to have absorbed mystical entities into his works, which show humans, animals and terrifying spirits transforming from one into the other. His masterful creations depict practically every aspect of traditional life and beliefs, and are still sought by institutions and serious collectors throughout the world, though his strength to carve is quickly failing. It was Osuitok who revealed to me the meaning of what appeared to be a meaningless pile of rocks, and thus guided me to my *tukisiuti*, my pathway of understanding.

❦ ❦ ❦

MANY YEARS AGO, Osuitok led me to his camp—some 55 kilometres (35 miles) east of Kinngait—for the first time. Our journey took us through a dangerous narrows at Itiliardjuk, where travellers would wait if they missed high tide. Well before we reached the narrows, I began to see inuksuit appearing on crests of hills along the coast, and I was told that some of these human-built stone figures had been standing there since the time of the Tunniit, the people whom the Inuit believe preceded them several hundred years ago. I was told that an inuksuk implies an object acting in the capacity of a human being, an Inuk (singular of Inuit), and served many purposes.

Approaching the narrows was an unforgettable experience. The water beneath the boat became threatening; we could actually see powerful currents rising to the surface to form whirlpools whose languid turns belied their dangerous nature. The buzz of fear was strangely exhilarating as we pushed against the sea pouring through the narrow gap. Huge submerged boulders unexpectedly loomed up from the bottom; we twisted and turned and suddenly broke free from the grip of a tide being pulled by the moon.

After coming ashore at Itiliardjuk, we climbed a nearby hill to escape a gathering horde of mosquitoes. We sat at the foot of an ancient inuksuk, drank tea, and ate bannock and shreds of dried caribou meat. It was a beautiful place to be, this narrows. I could see what Osuitok described as *utirnigiit*, the traces of coming and going, everywhere. There were ancient tent rings, fire pits, meat caches, the occasional stone fox trap, temporary stone shelters and graves.

But the most dominant feature on the landscape were the inuksuit. It was here at Itiliardjuk that Osuitok began to explain the different meanings inuksuit have or, more accurately, the different meanings inuksuit can be. "See over there?" he said, pointing to two small inuksuit standing side by side. "They tell us that it's a good place to get seals in that area." Taking another swig of tea, Osuitok pointed to a tall lichen-encrusted inuksuk. "That one," he explained, "is to be admired because it is so old and large it must surely have been built by the Tunniit. Therefore, its name is *inuksuk upigijaugialik*."

I pointed to a cone-shaped figure standing far in the distance. "What kind of inuksuk is that one?"

Osuitok looked at me with a faint expression of exasperation. "That's a *tigiriaq*. Anyone can see it's no inuksuk but an old stone fox trap."

Thus began my lessons into what some inuksuit say to travellers who know their meaning.

As we were about to depart, I noticed a scattering of stones on a nearby ledge. I asked why they were there and if they had any meaning. I learned that they were an *inuksuviniq*, the remains of an old inuksuk. Osuitok went on to describe how that inuksuk would have looked and its probable age, as suggested by the pattern of lichens growing on its surface. He then provided an explanation of why it was there. A very long time ago, he said, a hunter came this way, hoping to get through the passage. He missed his chance and decided to wait for the next high tide. Maybe he saw a caribou and pursued it. In any case, he had a long wait. Inuksuit tend to be plentiful at places were people have waited, Osuitok said. Some were built for a purpose, while others were made to pass the time. It's at the waiting places where you can sometimes find an *inuksuapik*, Osuitok said, the most beautiful kind of inuksuk. It is built with the greatest care, and its shape, as well as the colour or texture of the stones, causes it to stand out from all the others.

➤ ➤ ➤

TIMELESS MESSAGES FROM A DISTANT PAST.
SOME ARE EXAMPLES OF TYPES AND FUNCTIONS OF INUKSUIT (PLURAL OF INUKSUK),
MEANING "TO ACT IN THE CAPACITY OF A HUMAN."
OTHERS RESEMBLE OR APPEAR TO BE INUKSUIT BUT ARE NOT;
THEY ARE INNUNGUAIT (PLURAL OF INNUNGUAQ), MEANING "IN THE LIKENESS OF A HUMAN"
OR THEY ARE OBJECTS OF VENERATION.

NIUNGVALIRULUIT:
An inuksuk in the shape
of a window, used for
sighting and aligning.
It either frames a place
that may or may not be
in view, or indicates a
precise direction.
This one is a sightline to
an important ancient
campsite at Nurrata on
Baffin Island.

INUKSUK TUKTUNNUTIIT:
An inuksuk that appears to sprout antlers announces
a rich caribou hunting area, near Alariaq Island,
Kinngait area, southwest Baffin Island. Sometimes
this type of inuksuk may be topped with moss
or feature scapula, driftwood and a caribou skull.

TUNILLARVIK:
This inuksuk-like figure is
often a single upright stone.
People left offerings in the
hope of receiving protection
from helping spirits,
Arviatjuaq (Sentry Island,
Keewatin region.

USUKJUAQ:
This ancient and universal
symbol of fertility
indicates a rich spawning area
and the direction
in which to find it.
The shoulder-high inuksuk
can be seen from afar,
interior, Keewatin region.

INUKSULLARIK:
This ancient inuksuk, fused with black lichen,
is believed to have been built by the Tunniit
(whom the Inuit consider to be their predecessors).
It is a very important ancient inuksuk and is
so venerated that even children are respectful of it.
This particular one is located on southwest Baffin Island.

IQALUQARNIRAIJUQ:
These specially positioned
red and black stones
on the shoreline of a freshwater lake
signify a good place to catch fish.
Usually placed by women,
this type of inuksuk appears to be
unique to the Keewatin region.

INUKS
INUKTAQARNIRAIJU
This figure resembling an inuk
sports arms and symbol
the presence of humans, perh
informing Inuit wha
of a meeting place, Itiliard
southwest Baffin Isla

TAMMARIIKKUTI:
The significance lies in the stone resting on top
of this existing inuksuk, interior, Keewatin region.
Such an addition made by a travelling hunter
tells his family following far behind that
he has changed plans and gone in a new direction.

ANGAKU'HABVIK:
An inuksuk-like structure where
shamans were initiated
and received their powers in
the Keewatin region. "I come to you
because I desire to see," were the
words uttered by the novice.
It is still regarded as an object from
which to keep a safe distance.

WHILE I WAS AMASSING plenty of facts and information about inuksuit, it never occurred to me that I was fitting everything I was experiencing within the confines of what I knew, how I had been taught to learn and how I was told the world operates. Fortunately, a little misunderstanding changed all this.

Sitting outside one day with Oshutsiak, I began to question him on how he found his way while travelling during the dark days of winter. Not knowing the Inuktitut name for Polaris, the North Star, I struggled to find a way to ask him how that heavenly body was used. I made a drawing of the seven stars in Ursa Major, connected each to create the shape of the Great Dipper and placed Polaris in its correct position.

Oshutsiak looked at the Big Dipper, and said my illustration made no sense to him. Brushing aside my irrelevant drawing, he proceeded to talk about the importance of Nikkisuitok. I asked him the meaning of the word. "It's the star that never moves," he replied. Aha, I thought, now I have my pole star. "How does one find Nikkisuitok?" I asked. Oshutsiak scratched out seven dots in the same arrangement as found in the Big Dipper, then started to connect them. He began at what we think of as the handle. He continued the line downward, describing the side of the dipper, then moved up and drew a line across what we would visualize as the top of the dipper, then down to the seventh star. "There," he said, "that's Tuktujuak!" meaning the Great Caribou.

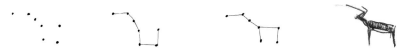

My Big Dipper was his Great Caribou. The constellations I saw existed for him in quite a different way. I was struck by the thought that perhaps there were countless things upon the landscape I did not see simply because I didn't know they were there.

The one time Oshutsiak allowed me to go beyond the barrier of his drawings occurred on a summer afternoon in May 1992, the year before he died. He, his son and I were on all fours, hovering over a map of Baffin Island's Foxe Peninsula. On the map, I had written the names of sites various elders had revealed to me over the years. Oshutsiak studied the map, and then gave me a rare gift: a description of a ghostly geography.

"Here," he said, "is where the the *ijirait* live, who are caribou-like creatures that can behave like humans. Over there are the Haunted Hills where the *turngait* (malevolent spirits) dwell. Up in this area living in the sea are a few ancient creatures that look like strange dogs. Beware of this place!" pointing to a particular inlet. "Evil things lurk about here." And on he went, sometimes pausing as if to reconsider what he was about to reveal.

By showing me where the spirits dwelled, Oshutsiak had brought them down to earth. And by causing me to look closely at the land with more sensitive eyes, he and my other mentors helped me see worlds that years before I would have missed. I could now, for example, perceive how an inuksuk, beyond being a tool for survival, could create a life of its own. Often commanding the crest of a hill so as to be seen from a great distance, a large and ancient inuksuk causes an amazing thing to happen. It creates the conditions for the birth of a microcosm.

Consider one such inuksuk I encountered not long ago. Standing atop a hill for countless years, it formed a windbreak, cast shadows, and attracted and held the warmth of the sun on its south-facing side. The shadow side was moist, holding onto the remnants of winter's ice

*Traditional Method of Caribou Hunting*, by Oshutsiak Pudlat, Kinngait (Cape Dorset), 1990. This is one of a series of drawings illustrating the use of *inuksuit tuktunnutiit* in directing caribou toward "shooting pits" where hunters were waiting. Such a place is referred to as *tallutellik* (where there are caribou blinds). The root of the word *tallutellik* is the word for shadow—one is hidden by a shadow. Oshutsiak has made many drawings of traditional hunting methods and spiritual beings, such as *ijirait*, the caribou spirits who behave like humans.

An ancient inuksuk such as this one
(described on pages 39 to 42)
can create the conditions for a
microclimate at its base,
Itiliardjuk, southwest Baffin Island.

and snow longer than the surrounding area, which had dried under the prevailing wind. Thus, the inuksuk created a microclimate, with its own temperature, wind conditions and humidity, within a one-metre (three-foot) circle.

Since it stood on the crest of a hill, the inuksuk had collected the signatures of countless birds over the years. The rich nutrients in the bird droppings worked their way down to the warm surface at the inuksuk's feet. One of the first colonists to arrive in this new world, as it were, was a tiny group of complex plants smaller than the head of a pin. The plants were products of a symbiotic partnership between an alga and a fungus, the alga cells interwoven with filaments of the fungus to form a plant body. Over time, the inuksuk became draped in shades of black, dark green and sometimes blazing orange of the lichen known as xanthoria.

Nothing was wasted; even the remains of expired lichens added to the rich nutrients left by birds. And on one early summer's day, on the sunny side of the inuksuk, an undigested seed carried there by an avian visitor sprouted, sending down its roots into a teaspoon-size pocket of organic matter—the beginning of the microcosm. Year after year, new colonists arrived, either carried on the wind or in the digestive tracts of birds. Pollen began to be produced. An arctic butterfly and a lumbering bumblebee discovered the tiny oasis within the endless desert of rock. And so, under the protection of an inuksuk carefully constructed by some traveller whose earthly journey came to an end long ago, a tiny universe came into being.

, , ,

EARLY JANUARY. The ice continues to grow strong, the food caches of those still living on the land are dwindling, and hunger is never far away. *Tatqiniqquaq*, the moon of the shortest days, has become *nalirgaituq*, the moon signalling the return of the sun. There is a longing to see and feel the sun's presence. It has been seventy-five days since she disappeared over the horizon, taking her shadows, sun dogs, rainbows and reflections.

The long absence of sunlight alters the perception of the Arctic landscape. The horizon's profile, the curve of a familiar hill or the distinct outline of a caribou, often are obscured. The edges of time itself seem blurred. During such periods, objects can appear suddenly in the distance or simply fade from view, neither preceded nor pursued by their shadows. The Inuit once believed that this was when the spirits came closest to earth. Yet, even during the darkest intervals, people travel great distances in search of food.

An old hunter living in Arviat confided the existence of a spectacular occurrence of light on the winter landscape—the mysterious *tautoquuq*:

"I'm not afraid to admit that I have been scared of things in my life. One thing that aroused great fear was when I found myself overtaken by the tautoquuq. It happened one winter when I camped by a small lake. I was on my way to get some caribou. I was alone because my partner was sick and dogs were too yappy to take when hunting caribou. Sometime during the night, I heard a loud crack that startled me. As I rushed out to see what it was, another and yet another crack broke the silence. To my horror, a great streak of light flashed through the ice on the lake, making a terrible crashing sound. Soon there was light flashing through the ice in every direction, followed by sounds that crackled and hissed everywhere. I climbed to the top of a small hill nearby, leaving my belongings behind, and watched this frightful thing until it finally spluttered and went out. I am not the only one who has seen such things. The thought of it still frightens me."

Once, when overcome by gloomy days and miserable nights, a friend observed yet another source of extraordinary light—the creation of a miniature sun. It happened this way.

He and his companion had waited out a five-day storm in their small igloo with only the feeble light of a candle to comfort them. When the wind died down and they could study their surroundings, they found themselves in a silent and forbidding place. The two decided to pass one more night there and then move on. In the meantime, my friend's companion, an old man, wandered off in the direction of the floe's edge and returned dragging a huge lump of ice. This puzzled my friend; they had enough water and he could think of no reason why the old man struggled to move the ice to within three metres (10 feet) of the igloo. Even more puzzling, the old fellow, buried in concentration, began to chop pieces off the ice block with a small hand axe.

Even with all the chopping and slashing, the ice assumed no recognizable shape. After some time, the old fellow, now armed with a screwdriver as well as a hand axe, opened a hole from the top of the ice block down to its centre. Having completed the hole to his satisfaction, he crawled into the igloo and re-emerged with a small candle, which he placed in the hole and lit.

A most curious thing, my friend thought—this lighting of a candle in a shapeless block of ice. The old man then walked slowly around his creation, humming a tune and seeming to be looking for something that, to my friend, was quite invisible. Without warning, the man grabbed his axe and attacked the ice with deliberate and precise

blows. At the last strike, it was as if a miracle happened. Light spilled from what was now a great crystal. My friend laughed in amazement. Surprised by his reaction, the old man laughed and hugged him.

I have recounted this event to other hunters but not one has shown me how to make such an ice crystal. I have often wondered: Was it something lost in the past or found only in the genius of a single man?

# SILENT MESSENGERS

LOOKING BEYOND the visible limits of their new settlements, the elders I came to know shared vivid memories of their traditional life and perceptions of their metaphysical world. They caused me to look beyond the visible limits of my own perceptions of the world. From Oshutsiak's mystical mapping to Pingwortuk's secret for staying alive, my arctic experiences created for me a new life narrative, one with many side stories, important characters and challenging turns. But the one distinct figure, the primary and most reliable reference point, was always the inuksuk. When moving on the land under all sorts of conditions, I regarded a looming inuksuk as I would a protective parent or a beloved teacher.

During my travels throughout the Arctic, I came to appreciate these seemingly simple stone constructions as a nuanced and once vital form of communication, a language as rich yet more elementary than the one in which I am communicating now. An inuksuk is a proxy for a human in every sense of the word; it provides comfort to the travel weary, life-saving advice to the disoriented, a focus of veneration to the spiritual seeker. It is a timeless language of the land for a people who existed on the land. As one Inuit elder told me, "This attaches me to my ancestors and to this place."

Such a landscape—perceived both physically and spiritually—consisted of a vast network of places where opportunities for both success and disastrous failure were often in delicate balance. An acute sense of observation, knowledge and precaution increased chances for survival, but a slip in judgment could mean lingering death. Try imagining a life, as elder Munamee Sarko described to me, continually on the move, killing every living thing you and your dogs could eat, such was the *taimaigiakaman*, the great necessity. Munamee and those of previous generations journeyed thousands of kilometres in a single lifetime. Many began while in the mother's womb, travelling by dogsled, in a skin boat or tucked into the deep, wide hood of the mother's parka as she walked for days across the tundra to the next camp.

Within this ancient survival system, inuksuit had a vital role, one that they continue to play, as I learned on a day trip I took with an elder some years ago. I was travelling with Lukta, the son of a shaman. Lukta was taking me to his father's old camp quite a distance from Kinngait because I was curious to learn why some people were afraid to go there. Heading off by boat with neither a map nor a compass, Lukta and I navigated safely through a dangerous narrows and across the yawning Andrew Gordon Bay (Kangisurituq) to reach the camp. After I finished documenting the area, we got back into our boat and began recrossing the bay. We were not far into our return trip when I noticed a white line approaching us quickly. I thought it was ice, but it turned out to be very dense fog, which overtook us within half an hour. The fog was so thick that I could barely make out the other end of the motorized canoe, seven metres (23 feet) away. Sharing my concern, Lukta shut down the motor and listened carefully. It was what he could not hear—the sound of waves lapping up on shore—that troubled him. He thought back to the time we had set off—when the sun was shoulder high (by my watch, 11 A.M.)—and estimated we had been travelling roughly an hour. He took out a package of cigarettes, removed the silver paper and folded it into a tiny boat with a sail. He placed it on the water, where it quickly drifted off. From its direction, and taking into account the time of day and season, Lukta knew that the tide was going out into Hudson Strait, which was definitely not where we wanted to be.

Lukta restarted the motor and continued in the direction opposite to the drifting silver paper. We would go along slowly, stop, listen, then continue. Listening was the most important thing. Then we bumped into an outcrop, something not indicated on any map we knew of. In the middle of the still dense fog, we quickly got out of the canoe, and Lukta looked around. He could tell by the presence of lichens that the outcrop was not covered at high tide. Aware that it would be all too easy to slip off the rock and fall into the icy water, we carefully sat facing where we thought the land would be and waited. Sure enough, within a few hours the fog dissipated, and we could see land facing us. The first thing Lukta did was to pick up some loose rocks and build an inuksuk, which he pointed toward the land. And in his mind he recorded the image of precisely what the outcrop looked like. When we finally returned safely to Kinngait, Lukta told his fellow hunters all that had happened; that if they ever came upon the outcrop out in the bay and saw an inuksuk made in a particular manner, it pointed toward the land. From then on, everyone who followed would have that reference point. It was simple, and yet what I had witnessed was what his ancestors and their ancestors had done.

❧ ❧ ❧

BECAUSE OF THE IMPORTANCE placed on inuksuit, their construction was rarely taken lightly. I often watched an elder studying a jumble of broken rock, without so much as touching a single stone, visualizing how one piece could fit with another. Only when the picture was complete in his head would a helper bring the selected stones to where the inuksuk was to be built. The figure that emerged was determined as much by the shape of the stones selected as by their arrangement. Since it was essential to shim and balance the rocks as they were put in place, often a wonderful construction came into being as the builder cautiously sought the centre of gravity to give his inuksuk a long life. Like a three-dimensional puzzle, the pieces fit together with such precision so as to be held in place by the force of gravity. Though they may be of varying sizes and shapes and perform a variety of functions, inuksuit are not only a pleasure to behold but are so well balanced and constructed that they can withstand the ravages of time and countless storms. *"Nakalanagu!"* its creator may exhort: May you stand forever! Some inuksuit have been standing for so long that generations of lichens have draped them in a green-grey shroud.

Inuksuit can be large, small, slender or squat. Some inuksuit are taller than the height of two men standing one atop the other; others, such as a *turaaq*, an inuksuk pointer indicating the best—if not quickest—route home, are no higher than the thickness of a slab of stone. Inuksuit tend to be about 120 centimetres (4 feet) high, roughly corresponding to the height to which an average man can lift a good-sized stone while keeping his arms close to the sides of his body. By contrast, inuksuit taller than a human are quite rare. The elders claim that such an *inuksullarik* (an ancient, very important and huge inuksuk built by the Tunniit, the predecessors of the Inuit), was constructed by the efforts of several men, often working from temporary platforms of stone found nearby. They appear in low vast plains so that they can be seen from a great distance in the winter.

The most common types of inuksuk consist of a stone placed upon a stone, a single upright stone, or a cairn-like structure created by stacking boulders. The nature of the local stone largely determines the shape and size of the inuksuk and how it was constructed. Rough, irregular igneous rocks and large flat stones of varying thickness allow for the construction of limitless shapes. Rounded boulders, on the other hand, offer the least possibility of variation in shaping an inuksuk; they can only be stacked into a pyramid. An inuksuk constructed of rounded boulders tends to be massive because of its base-to-height ratio.

Five general types of stone structures are easily recognized by even a casual observer because of their shapes. The first is the *innunguaq* (the plural is *innunguait*), meaning "in the likeness of a human." It is a human-shaped figure that resembles or appears to be an inuksuk, but is not. An inuksuk is "that which acts in the capacity of a human." In the old days, an innunguaq was constructed to tell whalers that Inuit were nearby or to express thanks for living in a favourable area. Though it is technically not an inuksuk, its distinctive human-shaped form is familiar to many, and in a somewhat abstracted form it adorns the flag of the recently proclaimed eastern Arctic territory of Nunavut in Canada.

The second is the most elementary kind of inuksuit, the *nalunaikkutaq*, meaning "deconfuser." It is often in the form of a single upright stone standing on end, reminding its builder, for example, of where he cached his summer equipment or where he was to meet another person.

The third group is the *tikkuuti*, a pointer: this can be made in different sizes and shapes, such as a triangular-shaped rock lying flat on the ground or a simple arrangement of rocks placed in a straight line, with the largest rock at one end grading down to the smallest at the other end, indicating the direction to be taken.

The fourth type is an *inuksummarik* or an *inuksukjuaq*, often rounded boulders placed to form the shape of a pyramid and noted for being a larger than average size. Easily seen from a distance, these large inuksuit serve as important directional aids at headlands, entrances to large bays or high hills.

# CONSTRUCTION AND SHAPES OF INUKSUIT

Single rock
put in place

One upon another

Stood on end

Boulders piled

Flat stones stacked

Stacked and balanced

Fractured stone bal-
anced and supporting

Fractured stone
supporting, symbolic

Rock's position altered

Flat stone pointing

Fractured stone/bone
sound-makers

Mixed indigenous
material: stone, bone,
wood, etc.

Mixed media

# ARRANGEMENT OF INUKSUIT

Solo

Side by side

Sequential

Strategic—
for hunting

Aligned

Random single/cluster

Formal

Finally, there are inuksuit that have clearly been used as private message centres in addition to their original purpose. At the top, there may be a stone, or at the base, an arrangement of stones, left by a hunter as a message for a follower. The message may indicate the location of a cache or where an object had been hidden, may signify a change of direction from an intended course, or may serve as a warning or a sign for the follower to go to an alternative location or to the camp of a relative. In the case where a hunter has lost a harpooned seal in shallow water, he may align two stones on shore, pointing to where the seal went down, in order to retrieve it later. The meanings of the particular configurations of these personal messages are known between hunting partners and often among members of their families.

As well as being stacked one atop the other, large slabs of stone can be arranged in a number of ways. They can be stood on end to form supports for a lintel, and thus become an elaborate structure rather than just a heap. A few inuksuit, referred to as *niungvaliruluit*, are constructed in the shape of a window framing a distant inuksuk, and thus are part of an ancient sightline. Such sightlines may extend to a star, an earthly place or an object of great importance. Many of them were alignments to places below the horizon; a small inuksuk would be placed in front of the "window" some distance away, thus resembling a rifle sight pointing to a "target." Such an inuksuk, even when aligned to point the way to a mid-winter constellation, may not have served a strictly utilitarian purpose. After all, experienced hunters would know the direction of the constellations. Rather, as Oshutsiak explained, alignments were often constructed by those who felt the need "to attach their thoughts" to distant and familiar places, especially when they were a long way from home.

Among the largest and most conspicuous inuksuit are those that direct the traveller by acting as indicators. Before a traveller embarks on a trip, someone who is familiar with the area to be traversed shares information on the appearance and messages of particularly significant inuksuit, sometimes in the form of a song. To knowledgeable eyes, indicator inuksuit can communicate vital information such as: depth of snow; safe or dangerous crossing places; where ice is dangerous in spring; the deep or shallow side of river; where there is plenty of game or where fish spawn; where food or supplies are cached; where there are good hunting grounds for seal, walrus or whale; hauling-out places for seal and walrus; landing sites for boats and kayaks.

Many other inuksuit are used as navigational aids that rival the up-to-date maps and satellite information used by modern adventurers. They can indicate the best route home; the position of the mainland from a distant island; the direction of a significant place inland, such as a ceremonial site; major transition points between water and land routes; and locations where fog is prevalent between islands. They can also act as astronomical sightlines, lining up the viewer to the North Star or the mid-winter moon.

In addition to indicating good hunting sites, inuksuit can be hunting aids, such as decoys built in the likeness of geese. The most prominent of such specialized inuksuit were erected to help hunt caribou. A number of them were arranged to form a drift fence that guided the animals to the shooting pits where hunters, armed with bows and arrows, waited. Referred to in south Baffin as *inuksuit tuktunnutiit*, these structures were usually only hip high. When in actual use as a hunter's aid, a large clump of plant material was placed on top, with a stone to hold it in place. The long tendrils of plant material would blow about in the wind, creating the appearance of an eerie creature looming on the hilltop, to frighten the caribou and drive them in a particular direction. Among the most striking of this type of inuksuk were those made to produce sounds. Such inuksuit often had bones such as caribou ribs and scapulas dangling from them so that the slightest breeze would cause them to loudly click and clack in the otherwise silent landscape. The racket would frighten the prey, directing them toward the hunters.

I learned of similar inuksuit in Nunavik (Arctic Quebec) that were referred to as *aulaqquit*, which literally means scarecrows or bogeymen. They tended to be somewhat more elaborate than their Baffin Island cousins. Some had the dried outstretched wings of seagulls dangling on sinew lines. They fluttered in the wind, taking on an appearance that threatened the caribou.

I have heard stories of inuksuit and innunguait being employed as a defence stragegy. According to one elder, "There were many inuksuit built at Ataniq near Arviat in the Keewatin made to fool the Indians [Chipewyan] during the time when we were enemies." Presumably, such inuksuit were constructed to resemble crouching figures when seen at a distance. Other stories tell of Inuit living on Little Diomede Island, in the Bering Strait, building innunguait that were covered with skins and given spear-like objects to frighten the plundering Inuit from neighbouring Big Diomede Island. According to the stories, the stone warriors succeeded in frightening their foes.

Of course, some particularly mysterious inuksuit have the capacity to unnerve travellers all on their own. One clear spring day, my friend Luke Suluk and his companion stopped near several inuksuit for their mid-afternoon tea. While they were resting, they heard a clear, sharp whistle. "We jumped to our feet to see who was whistling at us," Suluk recalled, "but only inuksuit could be seen. They were making

whistling sounds. I'd never heard of such a thing until one elder who I told about our experience said there were inuksuit that could make whistling sounds. The sounds we heard haunt me to this day."

In addition to innunguait, there are other stone objects or structures that may appear to be inuksuit, but which are objects of veneration. In the Keewatin region, an *angaku'habvik*, which indicates where shamans were initiated and received their powers, is still regarded as an object from which to keep a safe distance. *Sakkabluniit* were believed to possess spiritual power. And a *tunillarvik*, which appears to be merely a rock standing on end, is actually where people left offerings in the hope of receiving protection from helping spirits.

Considering the many different messages embodied in inuksuit—particularly as travellers' guides—it is easy to understand why their placement upon the landscape is as important as their construction. Navigational aids are specifically placed to be visible from a great distance, whereas inuksuit that point to caches often are hidden from casual view. Some are placed to be seen against a snowy backdrop, indicating to winter travellers an inland passage or a frozen lake where fish may be found under the ice. Others are situated on shore to be viewed from the sea, to act as reference points along a featureless coast. There are inuksuit that have been carefully arranged in sequences stretching great distances, marking out a particular route across an area complicated by hills, rivers and lakes. Some are formally grouped to define a specific place or to form a circle, which, in traditional times, at least, was a place of power that demanded respect.

❧ ❧ ❧

A napataq (an inuksuk
that is a single upright
stone, a marker with
variable meanings) is often
meant to be seen from
a great distance. This one
is at Kangisurituq (Andrew
Gordon Bay), southwest
Baffin Island.

THE NATURE OF THE STONE AVAILABLE
AND THE FUNCTION OF THE INUKSUK
DETERMINE THE SHAPE OF THE MESSAGE.

An inuksuk called a turaaq may be
as simple as a flat stone pointing to the best
(if not the quickest) route home,
Sugba region, southwest Baffin Island.

Left to right: A rare example of a niungvaliruluit (a window-shaped inuksuk for sighting or aligning); two upright stones on end, called *nalunnaikutait* (literally "deconfusers") and a tikkuuti (an inuksuk of stones in an alignment, pointing), on a small island in Kangisurituq (Andrew Gordon Bay), southwest Baffin Island.

Surprisingly, the widest variety
of inuksuk shapes are made
by using rough irregular rocks,
Kinngait area.

Flat irregular stones may be stacked into a wide variety of shapes to form inuksuit, Nurrata, southwest Baffin Island.

This beautiful little inuksuk, just knee-high,
is a rare example of a form between
an inuksuk and an innunguaq, on southwest
Baffin Island. It has arms but
not a fully developed human-like shape.

At Iglulik, a large inuksuk, whose meaning is lost, called an *inuksualuk*. It is made of thin flat stones stacked upon one another. Two others are in the background.

Round boulders limit t shape of an inuksuk to cairn-like structure kno as an inuksummarik, simi to this one on southw Baffin Island. Some may r to a height of three met (9 feet). This major directio indicator, placed at headla and entrances to large ba or on high hills, is usua meant to be seen from a gr distance. It may also point a place of importance, such where there are many cach

ELDERS SAY THAT the building of inuksuit began "in the time of the earliest humans, those who prepared the land for our ancestors." One legend from Labrador explains how the first inuksuk came into being. In the earliest times, a young man who had to depart on a long and dangerous journey felt a deep sadness at having to leave his loved one behind. Before departing, he carefully constructed an inuksuk, in which he placed his spirit to comfort and forever be at the side of his loved one. His love for her became widely known, and it became the custom by those about to take a long journey to build an inuksuk, which to this day contains the spirits of those who are gone.

Both in legend and in reality, men are the inuksuk builders, as they are the hunters who embark on long journeys and who are most in need of the information that inuksuit offer. But there are exceptions. In some areas, women make inuksuit called *iqaluqarniraijuq* of red and black stones placed together on the shoreline of freshwater lakes to indicate important fishing areas. And long ago, a number of women in the Kinngait area were summoned by a shaman to climb one of the highest surrounding hills, to gather the heaviest stones they could lift and to build a huge inuksuk. The women did as they were instructed, and when they were done, the shaman uttered an incantation. To the women's astonishment, their inuksuk began to tremble. Each stone settled firmly in place so that the inuksuk would stand forever.

When inuksuit were first placed upon the Arctic landscape is not known, but the first people to inhabit the Canadian Arctic arrived at least 4500 years ago. The oral history of today's Inuit refers to "ancient inuksuit built by those who prepared the land for our ancestors." The age of some inuksuit cannot be ascertained, either. Some old ones are constructed of a type of stone or are in an area that repels the colonization of lichens, so they tend to look recent. Others are favoured roosts of seagulls and other birds, whose rich guano encourages a luxuriant growth of lichen, so tend to look old but may not be.

My questions to elders about the age of various inuksuit and the occurrence of related events were often answered by situating the object or event in one of nine time frames:

1  Before there were humans
   *Suli inutagalautinagu silaqjuaq*

2  The time of the earliest humans
   *Inuit sivulliit tamaanigiagnaliqtillugit*

3  The time of the Tunniit
   *Tuniqtaqaliqtillugu*

4  The time of the Inuit's earliest ancestors
   *Sivuliriagnavut tamaaniliqtillugit*

5  Before the arrival of white people
   *Qallunaat tamaugnallautinagit*

6  After the arrival of white people
   *Qallunaat tamaaniliqtillugit*

7  Within living memory
   *Iqaumalugu taimagnanituqaluk*

8 The time when all Inuit lived on the land
*Inulimaat nunaqaqatatillugit nunaliralagnulutik*

9 When most Inuit moved into settlements
*Ilunagalatik Inuit nuumata nunalinut*

How do you read the meanings associated with such a variety of inuksuit? How do you know, for example, which type of inuksuk signifies a place where the ice is often dangerous at a certain time or where food is cached for winter? How do you know if what you think is an inuksuk is, in fact, not an inuksuk at all but some other object, perhaps one of veneration such as a tunillarvik, where people left offerings in the hope of receiving a favour, or the ominous angaku'habvik, where shamans were initiated?

The first step is to not think of an inuksuk's shape as symbolizing a particular message or piece of information. Apart from the window-shaped niungvaliruluit or a tikkuuti pointer, the shape of an inuksuk does not function like the shape of the letters that form the words you are now reading. Instead, they act as mnemonic objects, cues that are a reminder of some condition or particular thing of importance. To truly understand an inuksuk, you need three essential pieces of information. You must record in your mind every detail of the landscape and the objects upon it. You must memorize the location of places in relation to one another. And you must know the shapes of the inuksuit that are known to your elders, as well as their location and the reason they were put there.

Here are the instructions given to me by an elder on the placement and meaning of some elementary inuksuit before I embarked on a trip by boat along the south Baffin coast:

"Travelling along the coast eastward from Kinngait, you will first come upon an inuksuk that from a distance looks like a person walking toward you from where you came. He is particularly helpful in reminding you of the safest way home when the visibility is poor. Farther down the coast, when you reach the first island lying off to your left, you will see an inuksuk made from an old barrel with a stick pointing up from its top. Because this is summer, the inuksuk is only resting [in other words, of little significance]. The currents here are very strong, so be sure to stay close to the side where the inuksuk stands. But in spring, if you are travelling on the ice and see this inuksuk at the foot of the island [moved there by previous wayfarers], it means get off the ice at once! You may lose your life by ignoring its message.

"As you travel along the coast, you will see what appears to be a long low island far in the distance. In your mind's eye, divide the island into three pieces and head for the piece farthest away from you. As you get closer, you will notice that the waves are higher, the currents are stronger and what appeared to be a long low island is, in fact, three separate islands. The first island looks like a fat seal lying on the ice. It has a little inuksuk which looks like a finger pointing upward. The second island looks like an ocean swell coming toward you. It has no inuksuk. The third island looks like a long sled upon which is piled a huge load toward its back. There is an inuksuk here that cannot be seen as you approach. Keep going along the coast. There it is. This inuksuk is in the shape of a raven, at least from this direction. It marks the entrance to a little cove that can be easily missed. To your left is a single upright stone. This inuksuk marks the place of two graves. Keep to your right and as you approach the bottom of the cliff, look for a little inuksuk made up of three flat stones with a rounded boulder on top. This little inuksuk will lead you to the easiest route to climb the cliff and to the best place to gather eggs."

In similar fashion, my mentor Simeonie could describe from memory all the important inuksuit and other significant objects along the coast of southwest Baffin Island. He could relate them to specific places and describe their purpose. Had I possessed the faculty of acute observation and prodigious memory natural to him and his generation, he would have performed *tautcuunnguatitsiniq*, which means the conveyance of images to another person's consciousness.

While Inuit society has undergone radical changes over the past four decades, including the supplanting of animist beliefs by Christian theology, there remains a respect for the old ways as represented by inuksuit. The late Armand Tagoona, a charismatic Inuit-born Anglican minister renowned for his depth of knowledge of Christian and traditional beliefs, offered this account to me of a journey on the land he took after his ordination:

"My partner and I had been travelling by dogsled for some time. Each night, if I wasn't too tired, I'd read a little bit from my Bible, and each night my partner would mumble something about my new faith. And so it went. Approaching the Kazan River, we paid more attention to our surroundings, for this was a place of great importance to generations of Inuit. There was cause to be respectful where so many people had lived and died. There were many revered objects and places in that area. Coming upon a huge inuksuk with a great round boulder perched on top, my partner stopped his sled and refused to go any farther. To do so, he explained, would attract great misfortune if we did not show it our respect. He went on to tell me the story of how this inuksuk, which is called a *kibvakattaq* [great weightlifting stone], was placed there a long time ago by a powerful man just before his death. It was said that travellers thereafter must attempt to move the great stone on top of the inuksuk or suffer terrible things on their journey. Observing such a traditional custom is called *tiriguhungniq*.

"So there I was, an Anglican minister, standing before an inuksuk believed to have the power to harm the disrespectful. As you know, only the foolish take chances on long journeys, and besides, anyone who worked so hard to make such a big inuksuk should be complimented for his efforts. To the great relief of my partner, I performed the old ritual of trying to move the stone resting on its top. Eventually, we arrived at the family camp, tired, happy and well, as was to be expected."

Perhaps inuksuit have endured because they have a presence not only upon the land but also upon the landscape of the imagination. They are also objects that gain importance over time. For instance, it is common to find little pieces of stone called *tunirrutiit* tucked into the crevices of inuksuit—placed by other people, at other times, from other places. By doing so, they have shown respect for the object and have attached a small piece of themselves to it. A spiritual family has been formed.

The inuksuk is also the substance of legend and stories. Some old inuksuit are mentioned in *aya-yait*, the songs passed from one generation to the next to help travellers remember a series of directions for long trips. I once heard of a man, for example, who travelled some 1800 kilometres (1100 miles) aided by a song given to him by his father, in which a sequence of inuksuit in relation to the landscape was described in exquisite detail.

To some elders with whom I have spoken, the inuksuk is everything mentioned and more—it is a metaphor. It reminds them of the time when people were attached to the land by an unbroken thread of reverence, when they created great dancing circles, built fish weirs, placed huge inuksuit on hilltops, made traps to catch the most cunning animals, and communicated by rearranging or shaping fragments of the landscape.

， ， ，

DURING MY TRAVELS throughout south Baffin Island, elders guided me to many unusual sites, such as Akitsiraqvik, the great stone circle on the west coast of Baffin Island's Foxe Peninsula, where justice was rendered; Qujaligiaqtubic, the beautiful ceremonial site of the midwinter moon festival; and one of the most spectacular sites of the eastern Arctic, Inuksugalait (meaning where there are many, many inuksuit).

In the summer of 1991, Pauta Saila, along with his wife, Pitaloosie, and other members of his family and me, piled into an open freighter canoe propelled by a 90-horsepower motor and headed out to sea. After two days, landing each evening to camp, Pauta said, "Look, over there!" We were heading straight for shore. In the distance, I saw what appeared to be a jumble of rocks. When we landed, I was astonished. What had looked like a pile of rocks from a distance was, in fact, a great circle of upright stones.

This was Akitsiraqvik. Its name is so ancient that only the root, which means "to strike out" or "to punish," suggests its meaning. For countless generations, right up to the beginning of this century, Akitsiraqvik was where a powerful Inuit council met to discuss grave matters and to exercise justice. Its very existence challenges the generally held idea that the Inuit never developed a system of law or courts.

It is a place that even to this day holds immense power and is revered by the elders who know of its existence.

I slowly walked about the great circle, carefully looking at each standing stone and sensing the power of the place. I stood there awed not only by what I saw but by the thought that sometime in the distant past, someone as mortal as I caused this great structure to rise from a field of broken rock. Imagine standing on a vast, flat sheet of rock about the size of a playing field. At its centre lies a circle constructed of huge, thick granite slabs standing on their ends. The naturally formed slabs range from 50 to 100 centimetres (20 to 40 inches) high, are 50 centimetres (20 inches) thick, and weigh up to one tonne (1 ton) each. Seventeen in number, they form a near-perfect circle 6.7 metres (22 feet) in diameter.

At one end of the circle stands a single, massive, upright stone about the height of a person. Directly opposite stands an even larger stone reaching more than two metres (6½ feet) high. Within the circle are stone slabs forming a seating arrangement. At the base of the tallest stone is a seat suggesting the place where the most important person sat. The reddish granite has a patina of black lichen that gives the great circle a sombre appearance. On the periphery of the circle are naturally formed ledges creating a large, semicircular seating arrangement in the form of an amphitheatre.

As long as anyone can remember, Pauta said, this was an ancient place. People came here from all along the coast, but they never lived here. From the earliest times, this was where people held celebrations, where they played games of strength and skill, and where the camp bosses sometimes met to deal with matters of great importance.

Late that same evening, I returned to the great circle alone, approaching it from the landward side. It was silhouetted against the darkening sea, and I perceived not a circle but what looked like the shape of a ship sailing northward. The image of Pauta sitting at the head of the circle came to mind, as did an illustration from a reference book. It depicted a great stone circle much like the one before me. It, too, was a parliament where justice was rendered, and sitting at the head of the circle on a stone bench was the "chief justice." Surrounding him were other powerful men who sailed the arctic seas. They were the Vikings.

The ceremonial site of the mid-winter moon festival, Qujaligiaqtubic, is dominated by a granite "sugar loaf" hill some 35 metres (115 feet) high, at the top of which is a small tunillarvik, where offerings were left by those embarking on hazardous journeys across the treacherous Hudson Strait to the mainland of Canada. The entire site is sheltered by surrounding hills, making it an ideal place for gatherings. Qujaligiaqtubic is kept very clean, indicating the respect that the Inuit continue to have for the site. Modern-day visitors are met by a meadow of lush green mosses and wildflowers, nourished by the bones of countless bygone feasts. On the right side of the cove, high up on the cliff face, is what is believed to be a witch's cave. Children were warned that to be anywhere in the vicinity would cause the witch to lure them into the cave to be devoured. At the foot of the sugar loaf is a well-worn path, leading to the cliff facing the sea, that features numerous and unfamiliar stone arrangements. Peter Pitseolak, one of the most powerful bosses to have lived in the Dorset area, described an inuksuk that once stood at the end of this path. He said it was built long ago by a shaman and was a fearsome object because, at certain times of the year, various people had seen blood oozing from beneath its feet and dripping into the sea.

Inuksugalait, one of the most imposing sites in the Canadian Arctic, lies at the mid-point between the farthest traditional camp of Nuvudjuak and Kinngait on the southwest coast of Baffin Island. It is home to perhaps two hundred inuksuit of varying designs, half of them toppled long ago by polar bears and endless freeze-thaw cycles. Designated a historic site, Inuksugalait is ancient; its origins are mysterious and unknown to the elders. It is speculated that from the time of the earliest inhabitants of this coast, inuksuit were built here by people either setting out on a hazardous journey or returning from one.

Though the site covers only about 1.5 hectares (3½ acres), Inuksugalait has a presence much larger than its size. Coming upon it for the first time was a startling experience. As we rounded a point at a sea level, we came face-to-face with a legion of ghostly figures, looming from an upward-rising slope. Even the visual aspects of weather conditions seem amplified. When shrouded in light fog, which is prevalent in the area, the inuksuit offer a frightening welcome. A setting sun casts long plum-coloured shadows from each inuksuk, while the bright light of spring transforms the stones into dazzling crystals.

One of my most cherished Arctic memories is seeing Inuksugalait in early spring, when the scores of inuksuit were bathed in a soft amber light. It was a particularly quiet day; a storm that had passed through a few days before had driven snow against the inuksuit, creating fantastic and eerie shapes. I was very conscious that lurking somewhere nearby might be polar bears, fierce creatures that frequent Inuksugalait during this time of the year.

On one visit to Inuksugalait, Paulassie Pootoogook told me of a site inland on southwest Baffin Island's Foxe Peninsula that had many more inuksuit than Inuksugalait. I found it odd that such a site had no name, was known only to a few elders and was located so far inland. As Paulassie said, "It's somewhere in the area of the lake that is empty of fish and filled with ugly little creatures. It is east of the Haunted Hills." He went on to inform me that this was where people had waited for caribou and hunted with bows and arrows a long time ago.

During the summer of 1995, we attempted to find the site with the support of the Polar Continental Shelf Project, but were unsuccessful. At the end of that season, before leaving, I asked various elders about the mysterious inland site; few even dimly remembered accounts of it. Two years later, I decided to make another attempt. Travelling with Paulassie, friend Mark Pitseolak and pilot Steve Horton, I flew over the western and eastern portions of the Foxe Peninsula. The major difference between the two areas is that in the east are countless islands. In winter, the floe edge extends much farther out to sea; the myriad islands act as stationary hunting platforms and channels for the passage of whales, walrus and seals. Inland, there are large nesting areas where geese are so plentiful that, when in molt, they can be herded like sheep.

On our flight inland to the east, we followed the great migration pathway of the caribou, which the animals followed from Nettilling Lake in the north during the fall to their calving grounds in the midwestern area of the Foxe Peninsula. So ancient are these trails that the rocky outcrops are etched with the hoof marks of countless caribou. It was if we were reading the very signature of life on the arctic prairie.

After flying for about an hour, Paulassie asked the pilot, Steve, to take us down. On landing, Paulassie got out to scan the horizon in all directions, looking for a sign that might tell us where we were. At this point, the most sophisticated navigational system was of no use; Paulassie had to interpret the terrain he had seen only occasionally in his lifetime, translating a vision of the winter landscape into what it might look like in summer. With some uncertainty, he decided that we should head south. Steve reminded us that we had only twenty-five minutes of cruising time before having to head back to Kinngait.

Southward we flew, with the landscape changing little. We saw a few inuksuit on outcrops; one outcrop appeared to have glacial material scattered over it, but the lack of good light made it difficult to define the nature of the material. As time passed, our disappointment mounted and we fell silent. Steve said, "If we continue to head south, we'll be on our route home. Southwest will get us there more quickly. What do you want to do?" I asked if he could spare a few minutes and double back to the outcrops that appeared to be covered with scattered boulders.

The sky became lighter, at least bright enough so that we now could observe faint shadows where small outcrops appeared. I asked Steve to take us down as low as possible and to circle the outcrop. In moments we made out stone figures, and I squeezed the talk button on my headset. "That's it! Jesus Christ, that's it!" I yelled. "We've found it." Paulassie, a Pentecostal lay minister, was beaming, pleased that I expressed my gratitude so reverently.

We landed the chopper, got out and just stared in awe at the multitude of inuksuit randomly situated in all directions. What a sight it was. Wanting to discover some part of the place on our own, each of us walked off in a different direction. I eventually met up with Paulassie, who was building a beautiful little inuksuk to celebrate our good fortune and to show the land that we were thankful.

I found a *kattaq* (an entrance to a place of respect, created by placing two large rocks up on end and side by side) and passed through it, sitting within a natural enclosure. I recited a prayer, and Paulassie and Mark joined me and began a chant in Inuktitut, giving thanks to Jesus for guiding us to this long abandoned place. It was then time for business. I set out to photograph the more prominent inuksuit while my companions made a count of all the features on the outcrop. We counted 225 inuksuit, one shelter and one *tupqujaq*, an inuksuk-like structure in the shape of a doorway, through which a shaman entered the spirit world.

While I was photographing at the far end of the outcrop, the sky brightened and, to my astonishment, I could now see the outlines of inuksuit on another outcrop a short distance to the southwest. And in the opposite direction, I spied through binoculars a third collection of inuksuit. The outcrops extended over an area of some 2.3 kilometres (1½ miles) and were home to more than three times as many inuksuit as were at Inuksugalait.

I asked Paulassie if he knew of a name for this site. He said that his father, Pootoogook, had once hunted in the area but never referred to the site by name. I asked Paulassie and Mark if we could call it Tukilik (a thing which has meaning).

Tired yet ecstatic, we returned to Kinngait, where Paulassie announced our find to the entire community via the local radio station. But there were still two big questions to address: why was the Tukilik site located so far inland, and why were so many inuksuit concentrated on the outcrops? The answers lay in studying the area and knowing how caribou were hunted in traditional times.

Tukilik is situated in the middle of an ancient and still travelled caribou migration route that begins near the Great Plain of Koukdjuak.

Imagine this great path on which hundreds of caribou moved westward en masse in the fall. The females travelled halfway, then remained behind to have their calves while the males continued west to spend the winter, returning in the spring. Some 145 kilometres (90 miles) from Tukilik and still within the migration route, we had noticed a large pingo-like sand hill. The downwind side of the hill was perforated with numerous holes, in all probability indicating wolf dens. Here, in the middle of the route, wolves waited for the arrival of caribou.

A line drawn south from the Tukilik site would extend to the once rich feeding grounds of walrus, beluga whales and seals in the Sugba region, where outer islands acted as hunting platforms. The hunting cycle began and ended at the floe edge. Hunters passed by certain islands to allow migrating ducks and geese to lay eggs, which were gathered by women and children. As the floe edge retreated, the hunters moved landward, establishing spring, summer and fall hunting and fishing camps. Travelling farther inland was saved for later in the summer, when the mosquitoes were gone, the ground was firm, and the caribou were beginning their migration westward.

Armed with lances, knives and bows and arrows, the hunters moved into the Tukilik site and took up their positions on the outcrops, patiently waiting for the approaching animals. In those days, when caribou were hunted on foot, it was imperative that the hunting area be kept scrupulously clean and that any trace of the hunt be removed. A wary caribou can smell even a footprint. Such an ethic would explain the absence of food caches, bones and other refuse anywhere in the area. Guts and other refuse were likely dumped into the nearby ponds and lakes.

Two outcrops feature a tupqujaq, to show respect for the abundance of caribou spirits believed to inhabit the area. The third outcrop is the only one to feature a series of hunting blinds, in an arrangement I have never before seen. There were sixteen of them, forming a continuous line or firing range along the entire length of the outcrop. Each circular structure was about 1.5 metres (5 feet) in diameter and constructed of loose stones piled to a height that would obscure a hunter lying on his side, as was the practice in southwest Baffin Island while hunting caribou from a blind with bow and arrows.

And why does Tukilik have so many inuksuit? I believe they were made by hunters who waited for days and even weeks for the arrival of caribou. The inuksuit were largely confined to the outcrops above the muskeg, where the hunters could stay dry and where their scent would not spread over the migration route. Some were probably constructed as a form of thanks for a successful hunt or to leave a personal presence on the landscape, as Paulassie did when he constructed an inuksuk on our arrival.

Turning to my few living elders, I asked how they would describe an inuksuk that seemed to serve no purpose on this lonely site so far inland. Their reply provided me with a new category called *inutsuliutuinnaqtuq*, which means inuksuit that are created to shorten the time that one waits. The Tukilik site can be described in Inuktitut as *tuttunik utaqqiurvik*, the place where hunters gather to wait for the arrival of caribou.

A NUMBER OF STONE OBJECTS PLACED UPON THE LANDSCAPE
ARE VENERATED TO THIS DAY.
THEY WERE BELIEVED TO POSSESS SPIRITUAL POWER
OR TO BE THE ABODE OF SPIRITS.

Sakkabluniit (inuksuit-like stones that were
believed to possess spiritual power)
encircle and thus define this sacred site
in the interior, Keewatin region.

This kattaq (a structure resembling two inuksuit
standing side by side) marks the path
leading to an object of veneration in the
interior of southwest Baffin Island.

A tupqujaq, a large inuksuk-like structure
in the shape of a doorway,
through which a shaman entered the spirit world,
Baffin Island.

A niungvaliruluit
(a window-shaped
directional inuksuk)
frames a place of
great significance
or provides a sightline
to a distant place,
southwest Baffin Island.

A kibvakattaq inuksuk, an inuksuk-like structure
with an enormous weightlifting stone
perched on top, at the sacred site at Arviatjuaq
(Sentry Island), Keewatin region.

A spirit figure
in the likeness of a raven,
Baffin Island.

Two small inuksuit at the
entrance to where
the caribou spirits reside,
southwest Baffin Island.

# PLACES OF POWER,
# OBJECTS OF VENERATION

WHILE MY JOURNALS WERE FILLED with information on the various meanings of inuksuit, there was very little on the spiritual qualities of the stone figures, just tantalizing suggestions. The earliest account of inuksuk-like objects believed to possess a spirit or spirits appears in the remarkable papers of the *Report of the Fifth Thule Expedition 1921-24*, the Danish expedition to Arctic North America led by Knud Rasmussen. The following account, collected by Rasmussen, was offered by an Inuit hunter named Manêlaq:

> In Spring, when there is water between the winter ice and the shore, big shoals of salmon follow along the land just at Nuvuteroq, and they are speared with the leister and caught in large numbers. But one must be careful about fishing like this from the ice if one has no kayak; for once water appears along the shore and the ice in Qûkitlroq [Simpson Strait] begins to drift backwards and forwards before the changing winds, it might easily go out to sea.
>
> Once all the men at Kamigluk went hunting for caribou and only the women were left. The men urged them not to fish for salmon from the edge of the ice, but the women did so just the same, with the result that they drifted out to sea with the ice. Suddenly the ice went adrift and they dared not jump ashore; there was only one who took the risk, and she was saved. All the others went out to sea and were lost. So pitiable were their cries and screams out on the drifting ice that from a distance it sounded like the howls of terrified foxes.
>
> But when the men came home they sorrowed so deeply over the loss of their women that they built cairns [inuksuit] up

on the shore, just as many cairns as there were women lost. They did this because they wanted these cairns to be seen by people, and because they wanted the souls of the drowned women to be on dry land and not out on the wet sea. All the cairns at Kamigluk are from this event.

My early attempts to learn more about such inuksuk-like objects from the elders had met with limited success. Often, I received an outright denial that inuksuit possessed spiritual qualities, or I was given a charming story or a terrifying tale that nourished my imagination, conveniently leaving no opening for questions. More often than not, I encountered the side-stepping *"Ah-choo?"*: Who knows? When dealing with an outsider, this response enabled an elder to avoid risking the consequences of revealing important things without denying their existence.

But now and then I encountered an elder such as Oshutsiak or Simeonie who would speak of spiritual matters, of objects and places deserving much respect.

The term *inuksuk* can be used in a generic sense for a stone object or structure, whatever its name or particular function, that "acts in the capacity of a human." Equally important are figures that resemble inuksuit.

These structures do not include the many cairns and beacons constructed by explorers, whalers, traders, surveyors, or tourists. The inuksuit-like structures and objects erected by the Inuit are often found in places of particular importance, or in their vicinity. While they may have the human-shaped form of an innunguaq, or may look like a napataq (an inuksuk that is a single upright stone), or an inuk-summarik (a huge inuksuk constructed of piled boulders), they do not

"act in the capacity of a human." Their spiritual or religious function was rarely divulged. They are a physical manifestation of spiritual power, and many are objects of veneration. Some served to mark the thresholds of spiritual landscape for the Inummariit (the real people), who felt compelled to build them out of love, loneliness or fear.

Some mysterious inuksuit-like figures can be fearsome entities: the evil *inuksunirlik*, which may have been created to cast a spell; the *inuksuk assirurunnaqtuq*, said to be able to transform into other entities; the *inuksuk anirniqtalik*, believed to contain a spirit; the tunillarvik, at which travellers left an offering; the sakkabluniit, stones believed to possess spiritual power; the *kataujaq*, an arch under which the shaman healed or protected a person; the kattaq, an entrance to a place of power, such as a sacred site; the tupqujaq, a doorway through which a shaman entered the spirit world; and the angaku'habvik, where shamans received their powers upon initiation.

Other inuksuk-like objects and structures, including the human-shaped innunguaq, could have the sinister purpose of focussing a curse or openly displaying the absolute love of a person or place felt by its maker. "There are not that many real innunguait to be seen," one elder explained to me. "I have heard that your children make their own innunguaq in the wintertime. You call it a snowman. There is a special kind of innunguaq—I have forgotten its name—but it too was made of snow. This was a fearsome snowman because it was made by a shaman. It was made to capture the spirit of the person that the shaman wished to harm. Secret words were spoken to it until it possessed the person's spirit. Then the shaman would take either a knife or a harpoon and kill the snowman. I have been told that the person, even if he was far away, would surely die."

I heard another story about innunguaq from a kindly man from Uluksaqtuuq (Holman Island), whose mother and her uncle had been shamans:

"What I am about to tell you happened a long time ago. There lived in a small camp a young girl who was very beautiful. Her face, voice, behaviour and the way she could make clothing made her very desirable.

"Young men often visited this camp, bringing food to the girl's father, hoping that some day he would say, 'Take my daughter, you are a good provider. She will make you a good wife.' But the father was not able to part with his daughter. He loved her and she looked after the old man as if he were her child.

"Her father once gave her a special stone he called *inurluk*. This stone is most valuable because you can make fire with it. You make a small bed of dried moss and take the fire-stone in your hand and hit it against a rock next to the moss. Bright sparks jump up and fall into the moss. There is smoke and then the moss catches fire. The fire that jumps out of the stone lights our *kudlik*, which gives us heat and light during the darkest time of the year. The old man's daughter could make the fire-stone give out sparks better than anyone else and could start a fire faster than any man using a bow-drill.

"She must have been fifteen years old when a stranger came to their camp. He had the best *qajaq* [kayak] they had ever seen. His harpoon and all the other things that were in his qajaq were made in such a way that you knew he was a special person. He spoke softly, but he could be clearly heard. He moved quietly, but you could feel great strength in his every movement. He did not speak like the people in the camp, and they asked him where his home was. He gave the name of a place that no one knew, and said that it was a very long way from their camp. This stranger stayed with the people for many weeks, and everyone was happy because he was a good hunter. He could find food when others failed.

"One night, the old man said to his daughter, 'The stranger is a man who will always provide us with food, for he is a great hunter. You must become his wife; he will look after us when I can no longer hunt.' The beautiful young girl had strange feelings about the visitor. She knew that the stranger had often watched her, especially when she made fire. But her father told her that every young girl who has never slept with a man had the same feelings.

"The summer was passing. The weather was becoming dangerous at sea, and the stranger told the people in the camp that he would have to leave before the days became dark. He came to the tent of the old man and said that he must go. He asked the old man if he could take his daughter as his wife and promised to return with her when the geese came back to the land. He gave the old man much seal, caribou and dried fish so that he would not be hungry through the winter.

"And so the beautiful young girl was promised to the stranger. Before anyone was awake in the camp, the stranger took the girl to his qajaq, saying that they must leave now because he could smell a change in the weather, and they must get past the dangerous narrows farther down the coast. The girl said, 'But I can't leave without saying good-bye to my family,' and was about to cry when the stranger told her that he had made this arrangement with her father.

" 'Come,' he said. 'Get into the qajaq. Hurry, the tide is going out.' He grabbed her hand, and as he pulled her toward him, she screamed. She had looked into the centre of his eyes—they were not black; they were filled with fire. She screamed once more, 'You are Inurluk,' and with all her strength pulled away from him. He shouted a warning, but she fell onto the rocks by the shore. The stone she fell upon was the stone which makes fire.

"Even though this happened a very long time ago, the beautiful young girl is still there where she fell. I am not sure whether Inurluk felt a great anger or a deep love, but one thing is known, and that is he changed her into an innunguaq. That innunguaq will stand forever by the sea looking toward the sunrise."

⸳ ⸳ ⸳

FROM THREE OLD MEN in Arvilikjuat (formerly Pelly Bay), I learned that inuksuit could be vessels for spirits. After denying any knowledge of inuksuit containing spirits, the three elders then spoke of their youth, when they lived in small camps that were ruled by the camp boss and shaman. "Our shaman was an old man when we were boys," they said. "He could call on many spirit helpers when he needed their power to help him see and do special things. He could call the spirits of the dog, caribou, lemming, wolf and many other creatures to help him. But even though he could do things that were magical, he knew that he would soon join the Adlerparmiut, the dead people. He knew that he would die when we set up our spring camp. He told his son that he had a vision of dying, and he spent much time with him describing all the spirit helpers and each one's special powers. His son was never a shaman, but he knew that there was a reason for his father carefully explaining many things before his death.

"The old shaman died at our spring camp, just as he had seen in his vision. None of the old people go back to that place any more, not because they are fearful but because it would be disrespectful. If you were to go to that spring camp, you would see strange inuksuit. Those inuksuit are different from any others. The last thing that the son did to show respect for his father was to build an inuksuk for each spirit that helped his father. Each inuksuk is in the likeness of a spirit, and the hill behind the spring camp is where they live."

⸳ ⸳ ⸳

WITH RESPECTFUL PRODDING and patience, I was given ever more nuanced insights into inuksuit and their spiritual power. Visiting Kinngait a few years ago, I asked Simeonie to show me the places he knew. He pushed aside my maps, walked to his tiny bedroom and returned with a blank sheet of paper which he carefully smoothed out on his wobbly kitchen table. He reached into a tin can for a pencil. "Watch," he said.

And watch I did as he placed the point of the pencil at the edge of the piece of paper. His world began with a single dot. From that imaginary point, a line grew. Without pausing, Simeonie drew the entire south coast of southwest Baffin Island, a span of more than 480 kilometres (300 miles). At one end lay Inuksugalait, the haunting place where there are about two hundred stone figures. At the other limit of the drawing lay his beloved Ammaarjuak, the place of the ancient sod houses, where he came into the world. I noticed that, though his drawing resembled my map, there were seeming discrepancies in his vision of the coastline. Compared to my map, Simeonie's chart depicted some places quite large while others were rendered more insignificant. I assumed this was due to his age, but, as I would later discover, I was wrong.

Simeonie, whom I call *atatasiak* (grandfather), softly sang to himself as the memories of his world flowed out the end of his pencil. The blank paper was now filling with the favoured location of seals,

*The Coast of Southwest Baffin Island*, by Simeonie Quppapik, Kinngait (Cape Dorset),
1990. The large drawing is of the coast from Kinngait (far left) to Simeonie's birth-
place near Ammaarjuak (far right), some 300 kilometres (190 miles) distant. He
identifies the location of whales, square-flipper seals, walrus, small seals, fish and
birds. He also shows the migration path of geese and the reindeer herd once tended
by Laplanders (the people of the pointed shoes) at Ammaarjuak. The inuksuit in
the large and small drawings are symbolic. They are not meant to show the structure
of inuksuit but rather to communicate a variety of impressions. The three
small inuksuit in the small drawing (far right, top to bottom) are the type used in
caribou hunting.

ᑉᒪᐅᓇ ᐊᑕᑉᐱ

walrus and whales. He moved to the top of the page and filled in an empty sky with birds returning from their vast nesting grounds far to the north. His landscape was a lifeline between land and sea that we call the coast, where he and his ancestors lived for countless generations.

For the first time since he began drawing, he paused as if trying to make up his mind whether or not to continue. He looked at me, lowered his head close to his drawing and continued. Now, though, he engaged me in his journey. "There are many inuksuit along this coast. Among them are ones that have more importance than the others," he said, placing their likeness on the map. "Why are they more important?" I asked. "Because they are at places where one must be respectful." Old Simeonie was clever enough not to place the objects on his map so as to reveal their location. He simply strung them out across the top of the drawing like some arcane code. But he left me a clue that I only recognized the following year, while on another trip.

We landed at a wonderful site in an area called Kangisurituq, or the great inlet (Andrew Gordon Bay). This is an ancient site where it is believed a strange people once lived. Elders spoke of it to their children as a place where they must be very careful. Such a place of power was referred to as *aglirnaqtuq*, where strict custom is to be observed, a place where spirits abide. We walked about, careful not to tread upon graves so ancient as to be hardly visible. As if lying in wait, an open grave appeared before us, with a profusion of wildflowers still being nourished by the nutrients of a person no longer there. We discovered all manner of objects: stone shelters, food caches, two large ceremonial circles. But what held us in wonder and admiration was a stone portal. I had seen such an object only one time before, in the central Arctic, 1000 kilometres (620 miles) from where we now stood. We

Facing page: *Mystical Landscape*, by Pudlo Pudlat, Kinngait (Cape Dorset), 1990. Note the horizon placed in the foreground, requiring the viewer to look beyond. Here, the viewer sees landscapes within landscapes. Cross-shaped inuksuit stand at the places of the dead (upper left). Pinnacles are shown on the land and on a nearby island (upper right), marking the sometimes dangerous passages along the coast of Baffin Island. There is an "island" (lower middle) prescribed within the landscape by six inuksuit. Such "islands" or places of power may be prescribed by a single great dancing circle or may include a large area of several kilometres, which is forbidden to all. Pudlo has made many drawings of mystical landscapes; several have been exhibited at the National Gallery of Canada in Ottawa.

were on the threshold of the very doorway—the tupqujaq—through which a shaman entered the spirit world. A short time later, I saw that shape again, this time on Simeonie's map. I looked at the site on the map where the tupqujaq should be and found the clue Simeonie had left behind. Places of importance were drawn large, places of little consequence were proportionately small. His map illustrated the shape of inuksuit and various objects of veneration along a coast where each island, inlet, bay, point of land, dangerous shoal, safe landing, ancient campsite, place of power and unusual object had a name.

Osuitok taught me that even a scattering of rocks has a name. The faintest traces of comings and goings have their name—*utirnigiit*. Yet, I had not made the simple conceptual shift from how I had been taught to rationalize the world around me to seeing it anew, even if, for just a moment, reflected in another person's vision. That happened gradually as I began to try and understand the importance of inuksuit.

❯ ❯ ❯

INUKSUIT were my consuming interest. Each year, I headed home from the North with rolls of film and notebooks filled with stories and accounts gathered from elders and friends. It soon became apparent that I had to find a way to bring order to the information. I consolidated my rough and scattered field notes. I reviewed bibliographic databases and tried to arrange facts in various ways. I assembled the images into a rough storyline. But any headway that I made was just an illusion of progress. Contemplating the accumulating piles of information, I thought of the Inuktitut expression *angiarivaa*—he hides it within words. In real terms, I had done little to increase my understanding of what had been revealed to me about inuksuit over the years. I was adrift in a sea of detail.

Again, I reviewed all my information, the scores of interviews, the hundreds of pages of field notes, the thousands of photographs. If I could just describe the numerous configurations of inuksuit and their many functions, if I could annotate references that had appeared in the literature, surely I would acquire the insight that had eluded me. But no matter how I arranged the data, insight continued to be elusive. Where was that conceptual thread that tied all the disparate fragments of information into perfect clarity?

I will never forget one sleepless night during the winter of 1991, turning over everything I thought I knew about inuksuit, looking desperately for something I couldn't even define. Out of near exhaustion, the memory of one moment finally emerged from the clutter. It was the recollection of a discussion with Osuitok about states of mind. I jumped out of bed, brewed a cup of coffee and rooted through my notes until I found what I was looking for, and in my mind listened to Osuitok speaking one endless night long ago. I began to read:

"The three of us were tired. It was late and we could hear the rain on the roof. It was time for the last cup of tea. We sat silent for awhile and then he said, 'You seem disappointed. Haven't I told you enough?'

"I replied that he had told me much about ways of thinking, seeing and dreaming but that perhaps we had missed something along the way. I said casually, 'Perhaps there is a state of mind that goes beyond dreaming that is so difficult to express that we seldom talk about it. Perhaps all these questions that I have been asking you are really childish.' Osuitok's eyes lit up and he sat on the edge of the sofa. Leaning toward me, he lowered his voice as if to begin unwrapping a secret.

"'Yes, there is a state of mind beyond dreaming. It is called *quiinuinaqtuk*. It is like a window through which one can see into things as never before. It's as if you have moved out of the tiny space you occupy in this world and can see the world whole and can see past its shadows. There are five shades in this state of mind, each one different, each one lighting the fire of powerful thought.

"'There is *qiinuituk*. This is when you are alone, the only living thing far away from earthly things and filled with peace. This sense of peace fills every corner of your mind. It is more satisfying that any joy you have experienced in your conscious life because it runs deeper than happiness. It can mend broken thoughts and feelings, and having experienced it gives you the knowledge that it can come again when you feel there is nowhere to go.

"'There is *angnatsiaq*. Because you and I are men, I will describe it to you as a man. This is the state of mind when you think deeply of a woman. No, it is not thinking about making love to her or her earthly charms. It is thinking about her as a beautiful and totally necessary part of your life. Her smell, touch, voice, movement and presence are as important to you as is your breathing. She is ageless. The both of you ensure each other's survival and in the bottom of your hearts you know that you will travel together forever. She is that one missing part of you that has made you a whole person. Every sunrise begins in her eyes.

"'Then there is *angutiisiaq*. How can I describe this to you? There are certain people who are known by all others as special people because they do everything well. They make the best things. They are the best hunters because they know the behaviour of animals, weather, seasons, tides and other things better than anyone else. It is not that they strive to be better than their neighbours. It is that they have a state of mind that does not allow them to do things in an ordinary way. They are compelled to do the simplest things as perfectly as can be done by a human being. Sometimes when you come across an ancient campsite you may find a cooking pot or harpoon tip that is the most beautiful thing you have ever seen. Yes, even an old cooking pot can be a special thing if made by a special person. The important thing to remember is that this state of mind doesn't mean that you can do just one thing—it is a way of living.

"'There is a state of mind called *siilatujuk*. I find this hard to describe because it happens to me. It is that state of mind that allows me to see a different world which is my very own place. Here, I am not subject to unnatural forces. Here, I can create things that are beautiful and that give me great pleasure. It is a very strange place because you know that it can never be, yet when you leave it and come back to the world we know, you discover that you have created a beautiful thing that you have brought back with you. I am a carver, so I bring forth carvings—but there are songs, stories and magical things that have been brought back by others from their own worlds.

"'Now I come to *issumatujuk*. This is a state of mind that allows you to think deeply of many things. Our minds move from thought to thought, hardly stopping to turn one over to see what the underside looks like. We say ah-choo because it is easier to leave behind the things that are hard to understand. There are riddles, puzzles and secrets everywhere. Some things that appear to be simple are complicated things in disguise, and so it is the other way too. To think deeply of things is not day-dreaming. It is moving through shadows, never staying in one place forever.'"

❧ ❧ ❧

THE ARCTIC STONE FIGURES MOST FAMILIAR TO SOUTHERNERS
ARE CALLED INNUNGUAIT, MEANING "IN THE LIKENESS OF A HUMAN."
THEY ARE NOT, HOWEVER, INUKSUIT,
MEANING "TO ACT IN THE CAPACITY OF A HUMAN."

A recently constructed innunguaq
(singular of innunguait)
facing the waters of Hudson Strait.

This simple vertical stone,
normally referred to as a napataq
(an inuksuk that is a single
upright stone, indicating direction),
is also a rare, naturally formed
innunguaq, at Inuksugalait, southwest
Baffin Island.

An ancient innunguaq points
to a companion inuksuk
at the beginning of an inland trail,
south Baffin Island.

This little innunguaq l[...]
like a lone fi[...]
walking along the [...]
near Tellik I[...]
southwest Baffin Isl[...]

Far inland in the Keewatin region,
an ancient innunguaq points to a place
where people must show great respect.

A single stone that in winter looks like
two figures. This is an inuksuk assirurunnaqtuq,
an inuksuk-like object capable of
transforming itself into other entities, at
Inuksugalait, southwest Baffin Island.

Three innunguait that resemble seated figures
once acted as a hunting blind
in the interior of southwest Baffin Island.

MOVING THROUGH SHADOWS. Putting aside the notes containing Osuitok's observations, I sat back and started thinking about inuksuit as more than just material entities. What was that "underside" of a thought of which Osuitok spoke? Could it be that an object, in this case an inuksuk, was simply the manifestation of its meaning? I went back to the countless notes, to the stories, to the names, to the relationships, to every single reference to inuksuit made by the elders I have known. A different perception was beginning to emerge.

By writing down the Inuktitut words and expressions associated with inuksuit and arranging these into related groups, I hoped to find meanings and connections that had so far eluded me. Linguists refer to such groups as semantic sets; a number of such related sets is called a semantic field. A semantic field is like a family tree, which contains names, dates, relationships and details of individuals. Within a family tree are subdivisions into either maternal or paternal descendants; these subdivisions are a form of semantic set.

Just as semantic sets and fields are useful to set out and understand family structure, so too are they useful to understand words related to any area of human experience. In the case of hunting, for example, semantic sets may include observable and non-observable entities related to hunting such as a particular form of inuksuit, hunting equipment, techniques, precautions, animal behaviour and religious practices or ethics. In this way, it is possible to lay out an entire network of meanings, each offering a particular insight into that transaction between life and death we call hunting.

More important, we can comprehend the relationships between visible and non-visible entities such as an inuksuk and an inuksuk anirniqtalik (an inuksuk containing a spirit). The semantic set can range from the highest order of abstraction (a meaningful thing) to a general entity (an object made by a human), then to the object's meaning (an inuksuk that warns of a dangerous place) and, finally, to fuller details of meaning (an inuksuk that warns of a dangerous place during the highest tides of spring).

Making up semantic sets also helps to distinguish between the literal and metaphorical terms, and to determine whether a word is an essential part of a set of words or merely one of little or no importance. For instance, following the path of the word angaku'habvik (a structure resembling an inuksuk, indicating where shamans were initiated and received their powers) on its "family tree" leads to the word *tiqiraatuq*, meaning "an arrival." In this case, the physical object—the angaku'habvik—becomes impermanent when referred to by a shaman as the tiqiraatuq. This is because the object in this context becomes a point in space and time where the shaman received his *angakkua*, his enlightenment, and thus acquired his *apirsait*, his shamanic powers.

Had I studied inuksuit as just individual physical objects, I would have merely documented their morphology and obvious examples of their use. By arraying all the information on inuksuit gathered from the elders and combining that with related Inuktitut terms and concepts, I was able to explore their underlying meanings.

❧ ❧ ❧

THERE ARE INUKSUIT whose meaning is rarely divulged to an outsider because their very names define the nature of the place to which they belong. Some of these arcane inuksuit, pointed out to me by mentors, often marked what we would call sacred sites, where traditions had been observed or where by shamanic decree no one could enter or trespass. Such sites were also where benign or malefic spirits resided; where shamans were initiated and received their powers; where persons were executed, murdered or suffered some other horrific fate; where celebrations, festivals, games, trials or communal decisions took place; and where offerings were made in hopes of receiving favours, protection or enlightenment.

I came to realize that often the only outward clue to the spiritual significance of a site or object lay in the meaning of its name, which reflected its personality or spirituality rather than its appearance. For example, the word tunillarvik (often an inuksuk-like single upright stone where people left offerings in the hope of receiving protection from helping spirits) not only refers to the object but also to the place the object occupies. I learned of this distinction on a visit to Arviatjuaq (Sentry Island). I was taken to where offerings—needles, tobacco, small carvings—had been left when people lived on the island many years before. The object to which people made offerings was a rather ordinary looking stone, a simple granite boulder that came up just above my knee. It was believed to have the power to protect those who showed their respect and presented offerings in the hope of garnering favours. I was told the name of the venerated object was tunillarvik. When I asked the name of the place where the object sat, I was told that it, too, was named Tunillarvik.

I had a similar experience many years ago while travelling with a long-time friend, Itulu Itidlooie, to a particularly beautiful place on Kinngait Island. Pointing to the unusual hill that dominated the site, I wondered aloud about its name. I was later informed that such a hill was called a *mitilik*, meaning a high rounded hill. Soon after, I learned that the hill was also referred to as the overturned kettle, and the place was called Igaqjuak, which means a great fireplace.

During my early travels, I had often tried to find Qujaligiaqtubic, the mysterious place where the mid-winter moon festival and other celebrations were once held. Its name is so ancient that it is difficult to translate. My friend Itulu described it as the place from which one returns to earth refreshed. All my attempts to find it failed, until many years later. This ancient site of festivals, where life was celebrated and bloodlines strengthened, turned out, in fact, to be Igaqjuak.

Eventually, I learned that not only places but objects, animals and humans could have more than one name. When I asked a wise old hunter the name for caribou, for example, I was greeted with the question: "Which name? Is it the name of a bull, a fully-grown bull, a bull yearling, a cow, a pregnant cow, a cow with fawn, a cow with no fawn or antlers, a fawn, a fawn shedding its hair, a yearling having just left its mother, a male whose antlers are beginning to grow, a male whose antlers have not yet emerged, a caribou of late summer when there is skin on its antlers, one in early fall when it sheds the skin on its antlers, or perhaps one in late fall when its antlers have the reddish cast of blood?" I realized then that the word *tuktu*, for caribou, is only a generality.

Words and their precise meanings are of prime importance, a fact that Osuitok regularly emphasized. It is important to call things by their right name, he would remind me time and again. Without knowing the entity's correct name, he said, how can one understand what it really is? Even though my command of Inuktitut was elementary, Osuitok urged me to gather words—especially old ones—before their meanings vanished forever. It was believed that certain words, especially ancient ones, contained the very essence of the entity they verbalized.

The most valuable ones helped me to visualize a new concept, a complex landscape, an entity that could be seen only by uttering its meaning, or some event my senses have never experienced, such as *kutanggirvaluk*—the sound made by little icicles being chipped by an ulu from the ceiling of an igloo as they fall into a dish.

Words and expressions are particularly important in order to "see" pathways, an important concept in Inuit culture. The Inuit world was once crisscrossed with many different pathways, some for travellers, others for shamans. I learned of *aqutitugait*, ancient pathways that led to routes of safe passage or to favoured hunting sites. Many were the habitual routes of animals that lived on the land, others of creatures living in the sea. There were also pathways of the mind—some led to wisdom, others ended in chaos. At some religious sites, only by leaving your footsteps on a particular path called the *apautaujaq* could you hope to evoke the spiritual powers latent in such places. I learned of a metaphysical pathway—*angakusarqtuq*—forbidden to ordinary humans, that acted as a communications link between shamans. And I was told of places, such as *inuktorviit*, where humans were thought to have been devoured.

Places of power and objects of veneration have a path, an *arquti*, leading to and away from them. There were invisible pathways not only to places of power but within places of power: their locations were rarely revealed.

When approaching a place of power, it is important to know where the pathways are—for entering, crossing, exiting. Not knowing the exact pathway to an object of veneration within a place of power can leave you wandering about on a temporal landscape. You can identify the sacred stone, the healing arch or the shaman's inuksuk—all

stone objects believed to hold power—but nothing more. The limit of your perception stops at the surface of the object.

❡ ❡ ❡

A DOZEN YEARS AGO, I had the opportunity to visit a Saami family in northern Finland. On the drive there, my guide stopped the car at a river crossing and explained that, as far back as anyone could remember, this was the very place where reindeer herders drove their animals across the river and to their summer grazing grounds. The guide pointed to a large rock lying at the base of a steep cliff on the other side of the river. "You see over there?" he said. "That's a sacred stone, a *seite*, where thanks were given for providing safe passage across the river." Fascinated, I told him of similar stones in Canada's Arctic.

In fact, as I discovered in my travels and research, objects similar in appearance to inuksuit can be found anywhere humans once conceived of gods, giants and sorcerers. The Andes have the *apashektas*, Nepal the *chortens* or *stupas*, and Siberia the *dorazy chaloveka*. References to standing stones similar to inuksuit indicated that they existed on every continent except Antarctica. One of the most spectacular examples is at Carnac in northwest France, composed of approximately three thousand standing stones. Then, of course, there are the dramatic megaliths and megalithic structures found throughout the world, the best known being Stonehenge in England.

There is, however, an essential difference in meaning between inuksuit and their related objects in the circumpolar world and the standing stones and related objects in the rest of the world. The cairns of the nonpolar world tend to be based on an egocentric view of reality, giving homage to death, victory, sacrifice, power, immortality. The language associated with inuksuit, on the other hand, is based on a survivalist view of reality. It is a grammar based on necessity—hunting to stay alive—where objects are not only venerated for their spiritual significance but are essential as a life support.

At times I have been tempted to place inuksuit in a larger global context. Fortunately, a dear friend—a noted archaeologist—cautioned me to "stay close to the Inuit elders and the North." He went on to admonish me by writing: "When you start comparing stone structures in the Arctic with those in Norway, Russia and Australia, then it's not too long until Stonehenge gets involved, and one thing leads to another. Keep the clarity of a northern vision and leave the rest in speculative limbo." I pencilled in the margin of his thoughtful letter, "Yes, Stephen, you're right." And so I got off the trail leading to speculation and sought direction from my elders.

How was I to know that several years later, the comparisons I was cautioned to avoid would be made by others upon attending my lectures at Cambridge and Oxford Universities in Britain and at UNESCO in Paris? A colleague at Oxford noted that the knowledge about inuksuit and the metaphysical landscape of the Inuit elders is vitally important for landscape studies, regarded as a growing body of research bridging archaeology and anthropology. She went on to point out: "Because most researchers in landscape studies at Oxford work in Australia, you gave them their first glimpse of similar work in Canada's Arctic."

Inuksuit have definitely struck a chord in Canada. In both the North and the South, they have become icons used to sell telephone and financial services, beer and sugared drinks. The figure adorns ball caps, sweatshirts and coffee mugs, and is much sought after as an objet d'art.

But here is the sad irony in the growing interest in inuksuit: the wisdom of their creators is dying off with the passing of each of the elders who once had lived on the land. On recent visits, I have begun videotaping the talks with my mentors, only a few of them still living, in order to create a permanent record that can be used by their grandchildren. But sometimes that is not enough. On a trip to Itidliardjuk and Kiaqtuq in 1997, I was dismayed to discover that an inuksuk I had photographed had disappeared while another lay in ruins. Once, whoever disturbed or moved an inuksuk was told to put it back exactly as it was or suffer misfortune or a terrible curse. To me, the collapse or destruction of an inuksuk that was a sign of welcome is like the loss of a close friend. Even if you repair it, it is not the same.

Perhaps feeling something precious slipping away, some Inuit are starting to fight back. When a Canadian brewery unveiled its beer label depicting an inuksuk-like figure beside a polar bear, an Inuit group decided to protest to the United Nations, asking the world body to recognize the inuksuk as the collective "intellectual property" of the Inuit.

There is no denying, however, that the Arctic I saw on my early journeys has changed. That was made clear to me in the spring of 1998, on a visit to Kinngait that swung from the profound to the sublime. As usual, I was warmly welcomed by my mentor Osuitok, who was in a precarious state of health. He spoke to me about life in the early days before the arrival of guns and missionaries. "These were times when seals, walruses, caribou and all kinds of birds were plentiful," he said. "They didn't fear us. We could get food close to where we lived. These were times when strange creatures could be encountered in the sea and on the land.

"All this began to change quickly as guns and missionaries came here. The guns scared off the animals and Uqammun [he who talks much, the first missionary] scared off the strange animals by his presence, or maybe it was just that we couldn't see them any more."

Osuitok then talked about how some Inuit hunted and killed the Tunniit, and how ancient words spoken by the Tunniit shamans were "kept alive" by Inuit shamans. "Real shamans never die," he said. "As long as there are people in the world, someone will believe in them. They are listening as we speak."

Then, as if overcome by some distraction, Osuitok switched course and began talking about how the magnetic North Pole was constantly shifting position, and how the earth had shifted on its axis. He talked about technology not as end in itself but as "a force or new ability" for humans to use to become stronger than ever.

A few days later, the Kinngait community held a late-winter festival, featuring traditional games, a fashion show and a snow-sculpting contest. The traditonal games consisted of the usual events such as high kicking, arm wrestling, thumb pulling, leg twisting and other assorted distensions of the human anatomy. The fashion show was a carefully crafted melange of Gore-Tex, caribou skins, Spandex, sealskin and Lycra clothing. The music ranged from traditional throat singing to the Crash Test Dummies.

The concluding event of the festival was the snow sculpture contest. Lacking the talent to render a polar bear, raven or sea goddess, I decided to construct in snow a replica of a traditional spiritual centre. I first prescribed a circle about 16 metres (53 feet) in diameter. Around the perimeter I constructed five sakkabluniit, stone figures believed to contain spiritual power. At one point in the circle I built a tupqujaq, a shaman's doorway to the spirit world, carved from a single huge block of snow. I managed to get two garbage collectors to help me put it in place.

Within the circle, which now represented an aglirnaqtuq (a place where strict adherence to custom must be observed), I constructed a tunillarvik, where people leave offerings when seeking favours. To complete the site, I built a facsimile of a kataujaq, the stone arch through which a shaman drew his patient in order to effect a cure. I was quite impressed by my efforts.

The next day, I spied the judges inspecting my aglirnaqtuq. They appeared puzzled as they walked about making notes and taking pictures with disposable cameras. Other Inuit visitors looked equally puzzled, and as the hours passed and no announcement of the winner was made, I began to fear the worst: that the community was beginning to think old Apirsuqti had lost all reason. Slinking into the little office of the welfare officer who counsels people in distress and who also served as judge, I blurted out, "Do you know who won the snow sculpture contest?"

"You did," she replied impatiently. "Your prize is waiting for you at the Co-op. Now get out of here; I'm going to a healing circle."

I dashed off to the Co-op, where I was presented with a huge yellow flashlight that required a battery as big as a brick, but I didn't care. My sacred site upon the hill had won first prize. When I awoke the next day and looked outside the window, the aglirnaqtuq had vanished; during the night, someone had destroyed it. All that now remains is a big yellow flashlight.

SIGNATURES OF THE INUIT
IN THE FORM OF INUKSUIT AND OBJECTS OF VENERATION
HAVE BEEN LEFT UPON THE ARCTIC LANDSCAPE
FOR COUNTLESS GENERATIONS.

Inuksugalait, one of the most
spectacular concentrations of inuksuit
in the eastern Arctic,
southwest Baffin Island.

An ancient sightline
between southwest Baffin and
Southampton Islands.

On pages 100–101:
Standing in the footprints of storms,
inuksuit at Inuksugalait,
southwest Baffin Island.

A innunguaq (right) and a tikkuuti
(an inuksuk that is an alignment
of stones, or a pointer)
indicate the way to Kinngait,
southwest Baffin Island.

The ancient ceremonial site
of Qujaligiaqtubic,
where the mid-winter moon festival
took place, Kinngait,
southwest Baffin Island.

On pages 104–105:
Lonely sentinels standing at
the entrance to Kinngait.

These inuksuit called *napatait* (plural of napataq)
are single upright stones that indicate direction.
Like strange haunting figures, they stand at
the entrance to a dangerous passage at Itiliardjuk,
southwest Baffin Island.

A beautiful inuksuk (meaning unknown) at a
revered site near Saatturittuq, southwest Baffin Island.

The mysterious figures
at Itiliardjuk,
southwest Baffin Island.

# EPILOGUE:
# IN THE STILLNESS OF
# THE MOMENT

An alignment of inuksuit from the coast
to the inland hunting grounds of
the Kinngait area, southwest Baffin Island.

EARLY APRIL. There are rare times when, even in the dead of winter, a violent wind is followed by a certain stillness. The sharp edge of cold is sheathed by a warm, strange wind. It sweeps over the land on its way to some distant place, in its wake leaving a beautiful ephemera.

It is now the season when darkness and daylight are of equal length, when seal pups are born. Though the sea ice continues to grow thick, the land begins to warm as the sun climbs higher in the sky with each new sunrise. Sitting atop a worn-down mountain, I notice how yesterday's sun has slightly melted the entire mantle of snow. Later, a cold wind would sweep up from a frozen sea and cast its chill, causing everything to recrystallize into a vast silent and gleaming landscape. For now, I am filled with a deep and overwhelming attachment for the land, *unganatuq nuna.*

The great stillness that enfolds me suddenly shatters. From the corner of my eye, I see a billowing, living cloud move across the sky, shaping and reshaping itself as if carried aloft by the wind. The cloud is the first wave of eider ducks following the path of the sun toward some distant open water. Soon geese and swans will follow. The red knot, a bird no larger than my fist, will arrive from Tierra del Fuego on its annual round-trip of more than 16 000 kilometres (10,000 miles).

But on this day, the first sign of spring appears on the land. It is subtle and easily missed if you do not look closely. There are countless small impressions on the surface of the lichen-encrusted rocks all around me. Some are no larger than a cup formed by a child's hands. The black lichen on their rims attracts the heat of the sun, which begins to melt the ice trapped within the indentations. Tiny pools of water begin to form, each bearing its own reflection of the sun.

Studying them closely, I can discern traces of minute plant life lying in wait at the bottom of each Lilliputian pool. I carefully bend down, touch my lips to the surface, and gently drink. The water of each pool, like a variety of delicate teas, tastes slightly different from the next. The first is somewhat woody, the second has an aroma of yellow grass, but this third one has the cool sweet taste of spring. The word for this moment is *immaturpuq*, when the earth receives its first water.

In the stillness of the moment, I am visited by the words given me long ago. "From time to time, the spirits seek us out because they are in need of human warmth for a little while. That is the time to listen very carefully to what they are saying because they are trying to tell us what we are really thinking."

An old inuksuk being restored by my friend Itulu Itidlooie to mark the end of our journey, at Itiliardjuk, southwest Baffin Island, 1991.

# APPENDIX: INUKSUK TYPES, FUNCTIONS AND RELATED FEATURES

## Variations of the Word *Inuksuk*

| | |
|---|---|
| *inu'ghuk* | a general term, Kazan River, Keewatin area |
| *inuhuk* | a general term, eastern Keewatin |
| *inukhuk* | a general term, western Arctic |
| *inuksugaq* | an archaic term for an inuksuk |
| *inuksuk* | a general term, eastern Arctic |
| *inukuk* | a general term, Caribou Inuit, Keewatin area |
| *inyukhut* | a general term, Coppermine area, western Arctic |

## Some General Types of Inuksuit

| | |
|---|---|
| *inuksuapik* | the most beautiful kind of inuksuk |
| *inuksuk quviasunnirmik* | an inuksuk that expresses joy, happiness |
| *inuksuk upigijaugialik* | an inuksuk that is admired because it is old and large and must have been built by Tunniit (whom the Inuit consider to be their predecessors) |
| *inuksuliaviniq inuungittumut* | an inuksuk built by a non-Inuk |
| *inuksullarik* | an ancient and very important inuksuk built by Tunniit |
| *inuksullariunngittuqinuksutuinnaq* | an unimportant inuksuk |
| *inuksutuqaaluk* | an ancient inuksuk |
| *inuksutuqaq* | an old inuksuk |
| *inuksuviniq* | the remains of an old inuksuk |
| *inutsuliutuinnaqtuq* | an inuksuk (with no function) built to shorten the time while waiting, such as at hunting sites or tidal narrows |
| *sakamaktaq* | a great inuksuk demonstrating the strength of its builder |
| *tunirrutiit* | little pieces of stone placed in or at an inuksuk, leaving a bit of one's self behind |

## Some Inuksuit Related to Hunting

| | |
|---|---|
| *aulaqqut* | meaning "scarecrow" or "bogeyman" or "flag," an inuksuk used to frighten caribou (in Nunavik, also known as Arctic Quebec) |
| *ilimasuuti* | inuksuit used to drive caribou toward water so they could be hunted from kayaks |
| *inuksuk aiviqaijuqarnir* | an inuksuk that signals a good place to hunt walrus |
| *inuksuk iqaluqarniraijuq* | an inuksuk of red and black stones that indicates a good place to fish |
| *inuksuk natsiqarniraijuq* | an inuksuk that signals a good place to hunt seals |

| | |
|---|---|
| *inuksuk qilalugaqarniraijuq* | an inuksuk that indicates a good place to hunt beluga whales |
| *inuksuk tingmaiqarniraijuq* | an inuksuk that signals a good place to hunt birds |
| *inuksuit tuktunnutiit* | little inuksuit topped with moss or antlers (sometimes featuring scapula, driftwood and a caribou skull), used to frighten and drive caribou toward waiting hunters |
| *pirujaqarvik* | an inuksuk that marks a meat cache |
| *ulagutiit* | inuksuit used to drive caribou to shooting pits |
| *usukjuaq* | an inuksuk that indicates a rich spawning area and the direction in which to find it |

## Some Inuksuit Related to Travel and Navigation

| | |
|---|---|
| *ikaarvik* | an inuksuk that indicates a good place to cross a river |
| *inuksualuk* | a large inuksuk made of thin flat stones stacked upon one another, a directional marker |
| *inuksuk nangiarautimik qaujimalitaq* | an inuksuk that warns of danger |
| *inuksummarik* or *inuksukjuaq* | a huge inuksuk made of rounded boulders, a major directional indicator at headlands, entrances to large bays, high hills |
| *itiniqarniraijuq* | an inuksuk that indicates the deep side of a river |
| *nalunaikkutaq* | literally meaning "deconfuser," usually a single upright stone standing on end |
| *napataq* | an inuksuk that is a single upright stone, very similar to a nalunaikkutaq |
| *niungvaliruluit* | a window-shaped directional inuksuk for sighting or aligning |
| *tammariikkuti* | a small stone resting on top of an existing inuksuk, an addition made by a travelling hunter to tell his family following far behind that he has changed plans and gone in a new direction |
| *tikkuuti* | an inuksuk of stones in an alignment or a stone that is a pointer |
| *turaaq* | a simple inuksuk that is a flat stone pointing to the best (if not the quickest) route home |
| *turaarut* | a simple inuksuk that is a pointer, one rock placed upon another |

## Some Inuksuit-like Figures

| | |
|---|---|
| *innunguaq* | meaning "in the likeness of a human," the familiar human-shaped stone figure mistakenly called an inuksuk (meaning "acting in the capacity of a human") |

| | |
|---|---|
| *inuksuk inuktaqarniraijuq* | an inuksuk-like figure that sports arms and symbolizes the presence of humans, perhaps informing Inuit whalers of a meeting place |
| *inuksuralaaq* | a little inuksuk-like figure made of snow, used for *nakataq*, a game of target practice with bow and arrow |
| *kibvakattaq inuksuk* | an inuksuk-like structure with a great weightlifting stone perched on top |
| *nappariat* | little inuksuit-like structures that hold lines on which to dry fish |
| *niptaniq* | an inuksuk-like structure, usually made of stacked flat stones, located at a place where people wait for migrating caribou |
| *niqikkuvik* | an inuksuk-like structure (upside down) that is a meat-drying platform |
| *qinngummigarvik* | an inuksuk-like structure to steady a telescope or binoculars |
| *tigiriaq* | a tall cylindrical fox trap that, from a distance, looks like an inuksuk, but is not |

Some Inuksuit-like Objects of Veneration

| | |
|---|---|
| *angaku'habvik* | an inuksuk-like structure where shamans were initiated and received their powers |
| *inuksuliaviniq angakkumut* | an inuksuk-like structure built by a shaman, similar to an angaku'habvik |
| *inuksuk anirniqtalik* | an inuksuk-like object believed to contain a spirit |
| *inuksuk assirurunnaqtuq* | an inuksuk-like object believed to be able to transform into other entities |
| *inuksuk nalunaikkutaq pimmariusimajumut* | an inuksuk-like structure that marks the place of an important event |
| *inuksuk nalunaikkutaq tuquvviusimajumut* | an inuksuk or inuksuk-like object that marks the place of a killing |
| *inuksuk pijunniiqsijunnaqtuq* | an inuksuk-like structure believed to have the power to heal |
| *inuksunirlik* | an inuksuk-like structure created to cast a spell |
| *kappianaqtuq inuksuk* | a frightening inuksuk-like structure |
| *kataujaq* | an inuksuk-like arch under which a shaman healed or protected a person |
| *kattaq* | a structure that resembles two inuksuit standing side by side, marking the path to a place of power, such as a sacred site or an object of veneration |
| *sakkabluniq* | a single large unusual stone or object that resembles a simple inuksuk and is believed to possess spiritual power |
| *tunillarvik* | often a single upright stone that resembles a simple inuksuk, where people left offerings in the hope of receiving protection from helping spirits |
| *tupqujaq* | a large inuksuk-like structure in the shape of a doorway through which a shaman entered the spirit world |

# BIBLIOGRAPHY

Ehrhardt, K. J. "Old cult stones and sacrificial sites of the Finnish Lapps in the regions of Lake Inari and Lijarvi" (in German). *Anthropos*, vol. 59, no. 5–6 (1964).

Flint, Rev. Maurice S. *A Workbook for the Study of Inuktitut (Canadian Eastern Arctic)*. Ottawa: Indian and Northern Affairs Library, 1991.

Kane, Elisha Kent. *Arctic Explorations: The Second Grinnell Expedition in Search of Sir John Franklin, 1853, '54, '55*. Vol. II. Philadelphia: Childs & Peterson, 1856, p. 159.

MacDonald, J. *The Arctic Sky: Inuit Astronomy, Star Lore, and Legend*. Nunavut Research Institute and Royal Ontario Museum.

Peck, Rev. Edmund J. *Eskimo-English Dictionary, compiled from Erdman's Eskimo-German Edition, 1864 A.D.* The General Synod of the Church of England in Canada, 1925.

Rasmussen, K. *Report of the Fifth Thule Expedition, 1921–24: The Netsilik Eskimos: Social Life and Spiritual Culture*. Copenhagen: Gyldendalske Boghandel, Nordisk Forlag, 1931, p. 379.

Schneider, Lucien, OMI. *Ulirnaisigutiit—Inuktitut-English Dictionary of Northern Quebec, Labrador and Eastern Arctic Dialects*. Québec: Les Presses de l'université Laval, 1985.

Therrien, M. *Le Corps Inuit (Québec arctique)*. Paris: Centre National de la Recherche Scientifique de l'Institut National des Langues et Civilisations Orientales du Ministère des Relations Extérieures, 1987.

Thibert, Arthur, OMI. *Eskimo-English Dictionary*. Revised edition. Ottawa: Canadian Research Centre for Anthropology, Université Saint Paul, 1970.

Vassilyev, L. M. "The Theory of Semantic Fields: A Survey." Originally published in *Voprosy jazykoznanija 5* (1971), 105–13. Reprinted in *Linguistics: An International Review* (1974), 137.

# AUTHOR'S NOTE

I am indebted to those who helped me understand the meaning of the words and expressions of Inuit elders, for without their help little of real value could have been collected and saved. There were amusing moments when my incompetence in Inuktitut would elicit gales of laughter, but never ridicule. "The great thing about our language," my Inuk friend from Labrador once said, "is that it can be understood even when spoken badly." Then he added, "If we wanted to."

In drafting this manuscript, I realized that from time to time I used words and expressions gathered long ago and from many different places. In the early days, I often wrote out words phonetically, as a standard orthography was still in development. I considered having the entire collection of Inuktitut words and expressions in this manuscript vetted and, where necessary, altered to conform to present-day usage of the language. I was encouraged to leave them be. To linguists, I apologize; to those who gave them sound, I express gratitude.

The beautiful drawings created by the brothers Simeonie, Pudlo and Oshutsiak were drawn specifically for the study of inuksuit I presented at the Canadian Archaeological Association meeting in 1992. The paper was subsequently published in the Archaeological Survey of Canada Mercury Series, titled *Threads of Arctic Prehistory: Papers in Honour of William E. Taylor, Jr.* I honour all four of these men, whose earthly journeys have come to a quiet end.

My first encounter with the
Barren Lands, Arctic Quebec
summer 1955.

Leetia Parr Itidlooie,
my early interpreter,
Kinngait, 1970.

On the land with
the Itidlooie family,
Sarko, 1987.

On the land with
the Saila family,
at Akitsiraqvik, 1991.

Osuitok Ipeelee,
my close friend, mentor and
teacher for over thirty-five years,
Kinngait, 1995.
Photo by John Reeves

Simeonie Quppapik,
my mentor of many years,
Kinngait, 1991.
Photo by Mike Beedell

With Itulu Itidlooie
during my explorations of
inuksuit at Itiliardjuk,
southwest Baffin Island, 1990.

# ACKNOWLEDGEMENTS

I sincerely thank the Inuit elders and others in the Arctic who enrich my life in many ways. With some, I travelled to places that had to be seen to be believed; with others, I travelled to places that had to be believed to be seen. The following is a recognition of those who, either directly or in some other manner, helped me to understand inuksuit, objects of veneration and the very land upon which we exist. An asterisk (*) indicates the deceased.

Baker Lake–Qamanittuaq (Far Inland): Martha Tiktaq Anautalik, Myra Kukiijaut, Arngna'naa, Norman Atangala, John Killalark, Lucy Kownak, Margaret Narkjangerk, John Nukik, Barnabus Perjoar, Hugh Tuluqtuq, Elizabeth Tunnuq

Cape Dorset–Kinngait (High Mountains): Pitseolak Ashoona*, Osuitok Ipeelee, Itulu Itidlooie, Kenojuak Asheavak, Ottochie*, Issuhungituq Qiatsuq Pootoogook*, Paulassie Pootoogook, Pudlat Pootoogook*, Pudlo Pudlat*, Oshutsiak Pudlat*, Simeonie Quppapik*, Pauta Saila, Pitaloosie Saila, Pauloosie Tulugak*

Eskimo Point–Arviat (Bowhead Whale): Margaret Aniksak*, Peter Aningaat, John Arnalugjuaq, Henry Ishuanik, Elizabeth Issakiak, James Konek, Andy Mumgark, Luke Suluk, Peter Suwaksiork, Leo Ulayok, Silas Ulinaumi

Holman Island–Ulukhaqtuuq (Where Material to Make Ulus Is Found): Wallace Goose*

Pangnirtung–Pangnirtuuq (Place of Fat Caribou): Jim Killabuk*

Pelly Bay–Arvilikjuaq (Place of Many Bowhead Whales): Three very old hunters*

Pond Inlet–Mittimatalik/Tununiq (Place of Mittima's Grave): Simon Akpaleeapik

Povungnituk–Puvirniqtuuq (Where There Is the Smell of Aged Meat): Tomassi Qumaq*

Rankin Inlet–Kangiq&iniq (The Great Inlet): Rev. Armand Tagoona*

Specialists who provided assistance:

*Guides*
Baker Lake–Qamanittuaq: John Nukik
Cape Dorset–Kinngait: Itulu Itidlooie, Jimmy Manning, Pingwortuk*, Marc
    Pitseolak, Peter Pitseolak*, Lukta Qiatsuq, David Saila
Eskimo Point–Arviat: Philip Tasseor
Rankin Inlet–Kangiq&iniq: Henry Kablalik

*Illustrators*
Baker Lake–Qamanittuaq: Ruth Qaulluarjuk
Cape Dorset–Kinngait: Oshutsiak Pudlat*, Pudlo Pudlat*, Simeonie
    Quppapik*

*Interpreters*
Cape Dorset–Kinngait: Pallaya Ezekiel, Salomonie Jaw, Annie Manning,
    Jeanie Manning, Nina Manning, Leetia Parr, Pia Pootoogook,
    Mukshowya Niviaqsi
Pelly Bay–Arvilikjuaq: Dolorosa Nartok

*Linguistics*
Iglulik (Igloolik)/Ottawa: Deborah Evaluarjuk

*References*
Eskimo Point–Arviat: Peter Komak, Eric Andee, Donald Suluk,
    Aniksarauyak
Povungnituk–Puvirniqtuuq: Tomassi Qumaq*

*Researchers*
Baker Lake–Qamanittuaq/Ottawa: Sally Qimmiu'arq-Webster.
Toronto: Linda Morita

My sincere thanks to the Canada Council and the former Inuit Culture
and Linguistics Section of the Department of Indian and Northern Affairs for
their support, and to the Polar Continental Shelf Project and the staff who
make it possible to explore remote and important areas with my elders. I am
grateful to professors William Cowan and Thomas Fotiou for introducing me
to the importance of semantics; to Charles Martijn for his undivided interest;
to Drs. William Fitzhugh and Stephen Loring of the Smithsonian Institution
for their constant encouragement; and to the late Dr. William Taylor Jr. for
his unequivocal support when it was most needed. Linda Morita's world-wide
literature search was deeply appreciated. Proulx Imaging Labs of Ottawa has
generously assisted in the technical aspects of my documentary work, and
Kodak Canada and the Kinngait Cooperative and the Hamlet of Cape Dorset
have supported my work for many years. I am indebted to Terry Ryan for his
assistance, northern hospitality and unwavering friendship. I am thankful to
have had the opportunity to work with Alan Morantz, the finest editor I have
known. I am most grateful to Diana Cousens, who keeps "the farm" running
and some semblance of order in my life, wherever I may be. At Douglas &
McIntyre, Saeko Usukawa offered much wise advice and guidance on the
manuscript and George Vaitkunas conceived the design of the book. Bringing
us together was publisher Scott McIntyre, whose confidence and friendship
will always be appreciated.

# INDEX